*FOUR WOMEN
IN A VIOLENT TIME*

Deborah Crawford

FOUR WOMEN
IN A
VIOLENT TIME

ANNE HUTCHINSON (1591–1643)

MARY DYER (1591?–1660)

LADY DEBORAH MOODY (1600–1659)

PENELOPE STOUT (1622–1732)

Crown Publishers, Inc., New York

Contents

The German-born science writer
Willy Ley once asked,
"Aren't there any other women
except those bit players Betsy Ross
and Molly Pitcher who had a part
in your country's development?"
This book, come too late to tell him,
is my answer.

Part I
DEPARTURES

1

The Great Mingle-Mangle

She was a sober child, even at play, skipping rope to the
chanting of rhymes made up by her elders to teach the books
of the Bible.

> Matthew, Mark, Luke, and John
> The Book of Acts then think upon
> Romans and Corinthians
> Galatians and Ephesians
> Phillipians, Colossians, then
> Thessalonians I, II, III
> One and two of Timothy
> Philemon, Hebrews, follows James
> I should know my Bible's names
> Lastly these of Peter and John
> Jude and Re-ve-la-tion!

Anne Marbury, or Merburie, was born on or about July 17,
1591, in the farmers' market town of Alford, in Lincolnshire,
England, the second-oldest daughter in a family of fourteen,

four buried in infancy. Her father's first wife died young; her father then married a certain Bridget Dryden—Anne's mother —whose grandnephew was to be the poet John Dryden.

Anne's girlhood was spent pleasantly enough wandering over the sandy hills of Alford, usually with younger sisters and brothers in her charge. From the highest point one could see the horizon line of the North Sea, six miles away. Three years before Anne was born, the British fleet had sailed home from the rout of the Spanish Armada, and Anne and the other children of Alford were still finding bits of Spanish plunder along that stretch of shore; most families in those parts displayed some salvage of the conquest—proof, said Englishmen, of God's preference for Protestants over Catholics.

From early childhood Anne was aware of religion, its presence felt in every aspect of daily life. Her father had been ordained a deacon, or assistant preacher, at Christ Church, Cambridge. At age twenty-two, with a magnetic charm, Francis Marbury used every chance that came up to thunder out at his congregation the fact that most of the people preaching in the churches in these times, the late 1500s, were unfit to guide their listeners' souls. In this, the long and fairly peaceful reign of Queen Elizabeth, the bishops of the Established Church were inclined to be tolerant of an occasional dissident voice, but the rantings of this ordained minister were too heretical; they clapped him into prison. Released a year later to resume preaching, he went right back to shouting the same seditious sentiments. Again arrested and now tried by a higher court, Marbury repeated his accusation: that unlearned fellows were being appointed haphazardly, for want of anything better, by noblemen, and were preaching the meaning of the Bible any which way to their credulous congregations.

Now Francis Marbury was silenced, forbidden to preach; while his daughter Anne was growing up, aware more and more of his frustration, and taking pride in the story of his

defiance before the threatening powers of the Church. Somehow the family made ends meet, mostly from money coming
from relatives of the Drydens. Anne never remembered going
hungry, and her clothes were the plain but serviceable garments of any child of a minister, farmer, or skilled worker. As
for education, she was taught reading, writing, and some figur-
ing, while her brothers went to the local grammar school.

Twenty-four miles south of Alford was the merchant city
that was the center of shipping in southeast England. Originally its name had been St. Botolph's Town, in honor of
the Church of St. Botolph, said to be the most majestic parish house in the realm; gradually the name was shortened
to Botolphs-town and then into Bos-ton. Anne's restless father
liked to visit Boston on his favorite roan, and so did ado-
lescent Anne, riding "pillion" on a seat behind the saddle. She
was always sure to be taken up in the church tower, called
the Boston Stump because it didn't come to a point, but as it
was nearly three hundred feet high, you could see the whole
town from the top and the ships standing out to sea—the herring busses from Holland that were rugged, square-rigged
ships of the fishing fleet; and other ships with cannon jutting,
setting out with passengers to explore the trading possibilities
with America, the New World. Daughter and father stood
in the cramped reaches of the spire and gazed until dizzy; the
girl was intrigued at the thought of herself sailing off to faraway places, but even more was she aware of the man's un-
spoken longings, to break out—to soar! Anne Marbury ached
to help her father, struck dumb in his prime, and had not a
word to express it.

When she was thirteen there was a boy down the road, Will
Hutchinson, gangly, freckled, with an anxious look and a wist-
ful smile. Five years older. Apparently he admired everything
he noticed about the buxom cheerful girl shepherding her
younger sisters and brothers. Will's father had a dry goods
store, and sometimes he would bring Anne's mother a length

of cloth, wool or linen, for her "to make something comely for daughter Anne." Anne smiled to herself while being fitted for a coat or pretty dress. How much nicer than if Will's father were, for instance, in the herring business!

A year later, Francis Marbury was given the chance to preach again. As he explained it to his long-waiting family, it was hardly a retraction of disapproval but an expedient; a minister had died and there was a shortage of accredited men without parishes of their own. And so not only would Marbury be permitted to raise his voice again in praise of the Lord, he would be raising it in London Town, at the parsonage of the Church of St. Martins in the Vintry. Anne got the message, if indirectly; her father meant this time to tone things down for the sake of his family and what they would finally think of him.

However, the main thing was, at age fourteen, she was moving to London! For the next few weeks, while her mother bustled and packed, Anne dreamed. What would a great city be like? And not only to visit but to live there, with one's father who would have his own church! She had never even imagined such a future for herself, and now it was going to happen.

Will Hutchinson hung around the Marbury house until the last satchel and valise had been stowed aboard the coach that bore the proud if rather shabby Marbury arms; then he stood in the road waving good-bye. Excited, curious, impatient, Anne could not spare a thought for the boy she was leaving behind. As she waved back, it did not even occur to her to invite Will to come visit her in London.

London didn't disappoint young Anne. It was just as noisy and colorful and exciting as she had heard it would be. Accompanied by her older brother Edward, she gazed at the spires and flying buttresses of the churches (including her father's) and the massive historic piles of Court and Parliament, glimpsed King James and his Queen riding out in a glittering coach, marveled at the profusion of shops that held treasures from Spain, the Indies, China, and even the primitive Americas—wherever England's ships had sailed—wandered in the section called Cheapside, the Street of Gold, so called because most of its shops were goldsmiths', and strolled across the great bridge over the river Thames also crowded with shops from which one could watch ships edge into port with flags one had never seen before. Also, there were miserable mews filled with screaming women and naked children, and bear-baiting gardens, and playhouses where the bawdy entertainments of William Shakespeare could be heard from half-way down the street; proper offspring of clergymen such as Anne and Edward were not allowed inside these places, but they could hover and soak up the exotic atmosphere! In that year 1605 they peered and ran and explored as fires razed parts of the city that dated before its occupation by the Caesars, and stonemasons labored to build anew the traditionally crooked streets that all Europe laid down to keep the wind from rushing unhindered along them.

And now that her father was preaching again, just being "home" was exciting to Anne. The Marbury rectory soon became a meeting place for clergymen from the Lincolnshire country as well as other London preachers eager to hear the opinions of a new man of the cloth on such matters as whether to kneel at Communion, eat the sacred wafers, make the sign of the cross in the ceremony of baptism, and bow at the mention of the name of Jesus Christ—was not that all dangerously close to the Catholic way? Minister Marbury held forth on the opinions he had mulled over for so many years—and his daughter Anne listened, and began to think of these things herself. Actually, for a girl with a lively mind, eager to feast on new ideas, religion was just about all there was to be had.

As the historian John Green put it, "All England was a church." There was no real science of astronomy, mathe-

matics, medicine; no botany, zoology, archaeology, no phi-
losophy, history or economics, no body of literature or
schools of music, painting, or architecture; even politics was
debated in the name of religion. England recognized few men
she called great. The poet Edmund Spenser's *The Faërie
Queene* was damned for its godlessness; the playwright Christopher Marlowe was stabbed to death in a tavern brawl over
his "lewd religious principles"; the actor-writer Ben Jonson,
stoned in some quarters for his barbs against religion in *Vol-
pone*, was tried for killing another actor in a duel and escaped
the gallows only by promising to be pious ever after; even
Sir Francis Bacon was later to be consigned to the Tower of
London. And gone were those royalty-licensed pirates, Francis Drake and Walter Raleigh, done in respectively by dysen-
tery and the headsman's axe. Across the Atlantic, upon some
freezing fjord, explorer Henry Hudson and his son had been
set adrift by a mutinous crew, never to be seen again. As Anne
Marbury herself was later to write, "There was nothing but
the great mingle-mangle of religion."

A second bitter battle was building between the Holy Roman Church and the Protestants, despite the fact that the first
one seemed to have been won for all time a century back. The
"Reformation" of Martin Luther had cleaved religious Europe down the middle, and cleared away the clutter—as he
and his followers saw it—of priests, bishops, saints, and Virgin
who had stood between a man and his need to commune directly with God. Shoring up the shaky new faith came another great reformer, a lapsed French Catholic, John Calvin;
and by the middle 1500s the Protestant Church would seem
to have been built on firm foundations.

In his native Germany, Luther's church flourished; in England, Henry VIII rebelled against Catholicism by having beheaded the wives he wasn't allowed to divorce. Upon Henry's
death his son Edward, then daughter Mary, and finally daughter Elizabeth ascended the throne; "Good Queen Bess" was a

Protestant convert and forbade priests to set foot on English soil; but the centuries of pomp and pageantry, ritual and ceremony that had bound up Church and State were too strong for her to break altogether—impossible to imagine reigning without one's Archbishop of Canterbury!—and so Elizabeth held on to her bishops. Protestants were still obliged to worship God at what they considered an immense remove, an autocratic filtering through the splendor of priestly vestments, singing of Gregorian chants and incantations of the Mass. In the forty-five years of Elizabeth's rule, her Catholic subjects bloomed but her Protestants languished, spiritually unfulfilled. They had been given a glimpse of the simplicity of worship toward which their spirits strained; was it to be denied them anew? And so, Protestantism itself was forced to split, and the Puritans were born.

At the beginning, these Puritans had no quarrel with the Church's interpretation of Scripture and certainly no desire to separate from the official religion, with which their whole lives were bound up; their only wish was to purify the way of worship. However, wishes expressed by grumblings and mutterings wrought no changes with an all-powerful and myopic monarchy; and by 1567, all over England little groups were meeting in secret to carry out services of their own selecting.

In 1603, the Virgin Queen dead, her nephew James was crowned. James found himself confronted with a Parliament comprised mainly of Puritans who proposed England be governed no longer by the divine right of kings but by a group of men elected to represent the wants of its people. The king's indignant answer was to turn the ancient body of law, the Star Chamber (so called because of the stars painted on its ceiling), into a secret court of judges, without jury or rights of defense, that punished with torture and mutilation those who dared differ with the royal decrees.

By then, however, the Puritans, mostly merchants and artisans, were powerful enough in their hold of the purse strings of commerce to force a confrontation with the king—later known as the Hampton Court Conference—at which their clergy pleaded for recognition within the Established Church; they were refused, but were placated by being permitted to take on the task of revising, or purifying, the Holy Bible; completed in 1611, it was destined to be known, somewhat ironically, as the King James Version.

But the unsuccessful conference had forced matters to a head. Now the battle lines were drawn, and many men became Puritans who had hesitated before to abandon the familiarity and safety of the religion they had always known. Anne Marbury's father was not one of these; he had fought his battles and lost them; now he clung to the third and last chance he had been given, and preached in his splendid vestments, and murmured Latin phrases to his complacent congregation. As for Anne, it was enough that her father was doing what he had always passionately wanted to do. But she heard of the Puritans and the uproar they were beginning to cause in a movement that history was to call the Puritan Revolution. A fiery Scots minister had seized the ceremonial gown of the Archbishop of Canterbury by the sleeves and shaken them, crying, "Popish rags, the mark of the Beast!" Religion might be all there was to fill a young woman's head, but there was no lack of excitement about it! Somewhat to Anne's fascinated horror, one of the translators of the King James Bible, Lawrence Choderton, wrote that even the Church herself "was a huge masse of old and stinkinge workes of conjuring, witchcraft . . . murther, manslaughter, robberies, adolterye, fornication . . . lieing. . . ." Anne wasn't sure of all the meanings of the words but they were certainly interesting. It was like living in the midst of a family constantly quarreling, a bit wearing, but Anne listened, and in the evenings pored over her own small Bible, solving any problem she might have in its "light of revelation." And when she was eighteen she made friends with a young woman in the congregation—just married—named Mary Dyer. Mary proved a fine friend to discuss ideas with, as she was at once both intensely serious and frivolous; she had intentions of becoming a Quaker—that was a sect that proposed to do away with ministers entirely—and she would like to design hats to be sold in her husband's millinery shop!

Anne didn't take Mary Dyer seriously but enjoyed her company in seeing the sights of London. For instance, in 1610, there was to be had for the seeing a sight rare even in this city, the crossroads of the world—"salvages" from the northern half of America. There were five of these salvages, men with copper-colored skin who dressed in rough leather garments and shaved their thick black hair into fetlocks and stuck feathers in it, and bore such names as (signs upon their bare breasts) "Nahanada," "Skitwarroes," and "Tisquantum." ("Salvage" was an Old French word derived from the Latin *silva*, "wood," and referred to the forests wherein these creatures were said to live; in less than a generation it would be changed to *sauvage* and then to savage. They were also called Indiennes and Indians, from the mistaken belief of Columbus, who came upon them while thinking he had discovered the western route to India.) But Anne was most impressed. And so, she could see, was Mary Dyer. Here were creatures of the forest who had never heard of Jesus, the Crucifixion, or Original Sin—and when they were told of all this, it was said, they paid it no mind!

In the year of Anne's birth, 1591, the first English colony of America, on what is now Roanoke Island in North Carolina, was wiped out by Indians; but Roanoke was already a late development. After Columbus had discovered the island of Jamaica and had become the first governor of Haiti—being sent home in chains because of his disastrous rule—next came John Cabot in 1497 to explore the mainland of North America. In 1513 Ponce de León roamed over the peninsula of flowers, Florida. In 1524 Giovanni da Verrazano explored the coast from the Carolinas to Canada, then, not satisfied, wandered south and got himself slaughtered and eaten by South American Indians. Fifteen fifty-five, and André Thevet accompanied one of the ships of an exploring party that led from South America to Canada; he described the Indians so accurately that by the time those five specimens were displayed in England they hardly seemed strange. In 1565 the first permanent colony in North America was founded, at St. Augustine, Florida. Meanwhile, Thevet wrote of the spreading influence of the French: "Ten leagues up the Penobscot River there has been erected a small Fort . . . there is a great Traffick of Skins." In 1602 Bartholomew Gosnold sailed over and discovered a commodity called by the Indians sassafras, which they said made fine tea for "curing wambling of the stomach." Gosnold explored and named a spit of land "Cape Cod," built shelters on "Cutty-hunk on Buzzards Bay," and returned the following year, carrying settlers to Virginia. Soon Gulf of Maine salt cod was being sold in London stalls, and English fishermen, dock workers, and carpenters were leaving for the New World with salt-laden holds and promises that their families soon would follow.

By 1604, with the arrival of a trader, Sieur de Monts, the race between French and English for barter and trade was on with a vengeance. A year later, Captain George Weymouth arrived from Plymouth, England, and along with fish and furs, brought back to England five Indians as curiosities to be put on display. The swarthy captives stirred the interest of the governor of the naval depot at Plymouth, Sir Ferdinando Gorges, who brought the Indians to London; there they were on exhibit for a time, but Sir Ferdinando assured them they would be returned to their native land—which they were, a few months later.

On the basis of Weymouth's enthusiastic reports, Sir Ferdinando went to the king and asked for a charter to finance expeditions to America. Such a charter, besides besting the

French, would meet the challenge of the Dutch East India Company, which had sent England's own Henry Hudson to seek a northwest passage to the unimaginable riches of Cathay (China). King James granted charters to the "London (later the Plymouth) Company" and to the "Virginia Company"—headed up by Gorges; and both began recruiting what they called "planters" for the plantations, or colonies, of America.

Young Edward Marbury, Anne's brother, wanted to go, but Francis Marbury wouldn't hear of it—the newly reinstated minister wanted no "pyoneers" making news in his family! As for Anne, no such ambition entered her head; she was content to be living in the exciting city of London.

In June of 1607, the first planters of the London Company sailed to the New World, landing at the place Weymouth had mapped out for them, Sagadahoc, at the mouth of the Kennebec River in "Main," the area so called because it was the largest chunk of the tract claimed by the English after the explorations of John Cabot. For their safe voyage, the little party held a service of "Thanks-giving" led by the Reverend Seymour, chaplain of the expedition and a friend of Francis Marbury. "We gave Thanks too soon," he later wrote, "for the Salvages were less than friendly." He arrived back in London, however, eager for another try. A few salvages were not going to get the better of trade-hungry Englishmen!

Next, Sir Ferdinando Gorges—who had earned the title of "Proprietor of Main"—obtained the services of an adventurer from the Marburys' own Lincolnshire, Captain John Smith. Smith had invested in the London Company's fast-rising stock, and in 1606 he sailed for the New World. By the time he returned to England in 1607, he had helped found the Jamestown settlement in Virginia, and had a tale to tell of having been rescued by the daughter of an Indian chief when he was on the point of being scalped. He and his crew had also brought back tobacco, "grown and used by the aborigines," and soon they were surprising Londoners by puffing smoke from their noses and mouths. In the churches such as Francis Marbury's the practice was quickly condemned, but nothing could stop the majority of men from taking eagerly to the new habit of smoking a pipe; tobacco shops sprang up overnight, and with them, small wooden statues of Indians on the counters. One shopkeeper had a life-sized figure carved, with a war club, or tomahawk, clenched in its raised hand and stood it in his doorway. But it frightened so many of his customers away, he finally had to have it chopped up for firewood!

And so, by the year 1610, ships were plying a fairly regular route from Plymouth, Boston, and other British harbors to the Virginia areas in America and up the coast to what Captain John Smith was calling "North Virginia," the area that extended to Maine. Stories abounded, such as the one about a fellow named Hardman Coombs who was found by a British frigate afloat in an open boat off an island in Maine with five women, no oars, and no idea of how he got there; and also about a Maine Indian chief named Worumbo, of the Abnaki tribe, who plotted to wipe out the white settlers hunting and fishing in his ancestral territory, but they crept up behind the local waterfall and pushed him over it. Down in Virginia, Thomas West, Baron de la Warr (later to give his name to the state of Delaware), had been elected the first governor of the Jamestown colony; and the indomitable Captain John Smith had been captured by pirates and injured but had escaped and returned to England. There was also beginning to be trouble between the London and Virginia companies over taxes; the Virginians sailed up the coast to the teeming fishing grounds, and the northern settlers demanded they pay Sir Ferdinando Gorges's company a percentage of the profits. This raised a howl in London, where Lord Chief Justice Popham ruled that "Jamestown must pay," even though the cannon on the Jamestown ships were effective in keeping the French from edging down the coast, while pushing them always to the north, into Canada.

So far the English emigration had been for the purpose of exploration and profitable trade. But in 1611 another motivation was burgeoning—the desire, in some cases the pressing need, to escape from religious persecution. Under the aegis of Bishop William Laud, the Star Chamber was growing more and more vengeful in its verdicts. This secret court was cutting off the ears of those who dared speak up for any Puritan beliefs, branding a man on both cheeks with the letters S L for "seditious libeler," and imprisoning others in filthy dungeons for life. It was enough to make a man like Francis Marbury quail and stick more than ever to the strict observance of Established Church ritual; it was perhaps also enough to set up an intolerable fear in him whenever he preached to his London populace. At any event, after only five and a half years of wearing fine vestments and lording it in one of London's most "Established" churches, Minister Marbury, in February, 1611, collapsed and died.

Immediately, the family was faced with the need to vacate the rectory to make room for a new minister. Anne herself was grief stricken. In the middle of packing up and confusion and tears, there was Will Hutchinson from Alford, hat in hand, a yearning bachelor of twenty-six. Anne was now twenty-one. What was she waiting for? The familiar, earnest face of Will Hutchinson looked very good to her, even though all he offered was a house back in Alford, where he had taken over his father's dry goods business. Velvets and tamsies and good stout Holland cloth that he sold around the countryside. Well, and would they not come in handy in making a home?

They were married August 9, 1612. Her father's will divided his small estate among wife and children, leaving Anne about £150, a dowry that went a long way toward furnishing a home. In May of the following year Anne's first child was born, named Edward for her brother, and baptized in the little church of St. Wilfrid's at Alford, where Will held the position of warden—responsible for the safety of the gilt-edged Bible, sacred articles of silver, and the locking up at night.

At St. Botolph's Church in Boston, a new vicar had been called, and was soon making a name for himself throughout all Lincolnshire. "Mister John Cotton," said one member of his congregation, "preaches an eloquent, even fiery, sermon, belieing his looks." The looks of Mr. John Cotton were described by others: "A stout, smiling little man." "Blessed with a generous mouth and a broad noble brow." Anne Hutchinson had always admired the church at St. Botolph's; now there was added another reason to hitch up the horse and travel the twenty-four miles to Boston on a Sunday morning. Her husband did not protest unduly. For himself, he would have been content with the local preacher, his new little family, and his growing dry goods business. But it's likely he sensed from the start his wife's need to seek spiritual nourishment from fresh sources. And above all, Will Hutchinson aimed to please his wife; sometimes he couldn't quite believe he'd won her.

The new vicar of St. Botolph's, short as was his stature, possessed a deep, resonant voice, and as he stood in the pulpit surrounded by the panels of gorgeous stained-glass biblical scenes, with a shaft of light raying down upon him from the high-vaulted window near the ceiling, Anne Hutchinson could not help but feel that they were well and truly married, the Reverend John Cotton and the church of St. Botolph. And yet, in point of fact, John Cotton, at the age of twenty-nine, had been considered too inexperienced and "lacking in polish" to be vicar of one of the most influential (richest) parishes in England. Also Cotton's supporters were said to have used something closely akin to bribery on the bishop. And so, if it hadn't been for an easily swayed bishop, Anne Hutchinson might never have met the man who was to change the course of her life.

2

A Fiery Covenant

"Ye warriors in Christ, be ever vigilant! Take up arms against the multitude of irreligious, lascivious thoughts that swarm in the air like a pollution, and the recurrence of Popery spreading the whole land like a plague of grasshoppers." Such exhortations rang out over the heads of Boston's landed gentry, who looked as if the only reason they would take up their flintlocks would be to shoot pheasant, or possibly poachers. But the force and color of the Reverend John Cotton's delivery seemed to make what he was saying a secondary matter.

Cotton's two favorite subjects were quickly marked as Catholic influence and the New World—to which, as early as 1614, he was urging members of his flock to fly, although at the same time he could hardly be said to be painting them a rosy picture. "The early settlers have been set upon by hordes of heathen salvages who killed them before they could even make peace with the one true God. Go! Avenge the repulsers of these Pyoneers of Christ. Hazard thy person in battle against these thousands of malignant enemies to bring about this new bastion of Christ's Kingdom on Earth in this Dismal Desert Wilderness."

There is no record that a single one of the phlegmatic landowners of Boston got up from his padded pew to go forth and book passage for the wilderness. But they all kept coming back Sunday after Sunday, like Anne Hutchinson, for the two hours a week that would lift them out of their ordinary lives.

During the next twenty years the Reverend John Cotton preached sermons that earned him a reputation extending beyond the boundaries of Lincolnshire and even of England. For her part, from 1613 to 1633, Anne was producing children at the usual rate for that age, one about every eighteen months. Three died in infancy; eleven lived and flourished. And during that time, Anne and her husband journeyed as often on weekends as could be managed to Boston to hear the silver-tongued orator Cotton. Apart from her reading of the Bible, the words of this minister were her only inspiration, stimulation for her mind.

Augmenting his sermons, Cotton would frequently hold informal sessions in the study of his "manse" next to the church. In these sessions members of the congregation were free to give their own opinions of Bible events—although only the minister had the "true meaning" because only he was in a "Covenant of Grace." This phrase pertained to the presence of the Holy Spirit that dwelled within a minister, through which he could interpret the Word of God—that is, the Bible. There were two Covenants that ministers held almost as tangibly as their New Testament or a communion cup—the other was the Covenant of Works. This pertained to the body of forms that man himself had devised with which to worship, forms such as prayer, baptism, and marriage. Most ministers Anne had heard preached a great deal of Works and very little of Grace—except for her father. John Cotton's emphasis on Grace reminded her of Francis Marbury. Both men in their rhetoric and range of ideas always seemed to be on the verge of turning into—Puritans! But there was a difference. In his third and last chance at having his own church, Anne's father had remained relatively orthodox; this was John Cotton's first chance, and there was not an orthodox word out of him.

Cotton seldom drew on Bible events for his sermon ideas. He believed in revealing God's hand in the world of the moment. In 1615, when the English Captain Hunt "tricked away from the New-England twenty-four salvages and sold the lot of them at the Rock of Gibralter for twenty pounds apiece, to see them led off in chains, was that not their just due, these creatures who live in God's world without serving Him?" The great comet of 1618 was second only to the Star of Bethlehem as a guide. "It travels from east to west, an harbinger of the God-blessed pyoneers to sail in its direction." And in 1618, with the outbreak of what was to become, all over Europe, the Thirty Years' War, Protestant against Catholic, Cotton really came into his own. A contemporary who heard him wrote, "Before this Prophet the Book of Revelation Paleth." (Perhaps this was the same man John Cotton himself mentioned in one of his books of sermons, *The Keys of the Kingdom:* "Taken from mouth in short-writing characters, and checked for veracity soon after.")

"Ye French!" shouted Cotton from his pulpit battlements. "Fear not the croaking of Frogs [Catholics] in your land; Christ reaches out his Hand to you. . . . Look what He has done for the English! Ye Germans that have had such a bloody Bickering! And oh Italy, the Seat and Center of the Beast; Christ will pick out a People for you; oh, ye Spaniards and Portugalls, Christ will show you the abomination of that Beastly Whore who has made your Nations drunk with the Wine of her Fornication. And you, the Seeds of Israel, the rattling of your dead Bones together is at hand. By Fires and Blood shall be destroyed Pope and Turks, when shall be seen great Smoke and Flames ascending up on high. For Christ the great King of all the Earth is now going forward in His great Wrath and terrible Indignation to avenge the Blood of His Saints, and now for the great and bloody Battle. Rivers of Blood and up to the Horse-bridles, even the Blood of those who have drunk Blood for so long, oh dreadful Day, when the Patience and long-suffering of Christ, what wondrous Works are now suddenly to be wrought." This vengeful aspect of Jesus was nothing strange to a woman of Anne Hutchinson's time, for she well knew the interpretation put upon the Crucifixion, as depicted by the painters, sculptors, and tapestry makers of the Middle Ages, showing Christ sitting at the Last Judgment and taking his terrible revenge on those who had betrayed him. And then, after such a sermon, Cotton would stand at the church doors, genial and relaxed, shaking hands and asking about a man's horses, his wife's health.

In 1619 Cotton was adding to the knowledge of Anne Hutchinson as to life in America by speaking of the "first legislative assembly in the New World" at Jamestown, under John Smith of Lincolnshire, and encouraging people to join the new, emancipated colony of Englishmen spreading the Christian Word. However much Cotton's sermons helped, emigration fever was at its height. Thousands of people (14,000 by 1624) poured into ships and set sail for the Virginia Territory or that of Massachusetts-to-"Main." Their vision was the fortune to be made, said those who had returned rich, in the fur trading and the fishing rights. Across the English Channel a ship's captain called Pourtrincourt gave Cotton his latest subject for a sermon. Landing at Cape Cod, the Frenchman had shot off his ship's cannon into a party of Indians rowing out trustingly to barter, as they had so often before with sailing ships. Then he had gone ashore and hanged some others, and left the whole place seething with hatred for any white men to come after. God would punish such Frogs making trouble for the courageous Planters who next ventured to land; and Cotton warned any who thought of making the voyage in the next year to consider locating in the safer territories to the south.

Shortly thereafter, in 1620, another group of about a hundred people did land in the middle of the blood-thirst raised by the French captain, but escaped the consequences by what Cotton was later to call a miracle. This was one of several small bands who sailed for different parts of the New World in that year—they were a "split-off" from the Puritans, a sect that called themselves Separatists. Separatists believed that each congregation in a parish should elect its own spiritual leader. This "take the law into one's own hands" belief, more heretical than Puritanism itself, had earned them special prosecution from the Established Church, and so a few years earlier they had fled to Holland. There they found that the Dutch, mostly Presbyterians with a united central church government, had no patience with them either, and so their representatives went back to London, and tried to obtain a charter with one of the companies with which to commandeer a ship for America. The Separatists did not sound like the ambitious planters whose energy in trapping and fishing would be likely to result in a profit from, or even repayment to, their London backers; so it took months of persuasion before they were able to buy stock in the Virginia Company and secure a ship, outfitted with provisions, with a charter that permitted them to take possession of a certain portion of land in the "North Virginia" territory that was south of the Hudson's Bay area. The ship was an eight-year-old man-of-war with twelve cannon, and she had made many trips to the Newfoundland banks; she smelled redolently of whale blubber and cod, and was one of three at the time named *May-Floure*. The Separatists were ferried out of Holland on another vessel, which proved unseaworthy, and at Plymouth the passengers from both were crowded into one. Arguments had not been settled about commercial terms and the group sailed without signing the charter; moreover, the ship's Master, Christopher Jones, had been bribed by the Dutch, while still in London, not to land in the area of "North Virginia," where the Dutch were, but to settle anywhere farther north. And so the Captain pretended that the landing near the New Amsterdam colony was too dangerous, and steered the vessel considerably to the north. In the region of "Cape Cod" the little party spent five weeks exploring this coast until they dropped anchor at the mouth of a harbor that Captain John Smith had named, six years before, "New-Plimouth."

Because of his interest in the religious motives for emigrating, John Cotton followed the progress of these Separatists, although not even he dared to call them by that despised name in an Established Church. He had hit on the name that people on pilgrimages had been called since the days of the Oracle at Delphi—"pilgrims." He was annoyed with these pilgrims for having landed in the very area where the French had left all those vengeful Indians; but God had provided a miracle. "The Lord sent his Spirit into the salvage, Tisquantum, and gave him the gift of the English tongue." *Now* would the people of Lincolnshire believe that "God's Spirit awaits you in this New Christian World"?

Anne Hutchinson recognized the exotic name of Tisquantum from having seen those Indians displayed in London. How strange to think of them now back in the New World. She wondered if she would ever see anything more of the world, or go on living in quiet Alford for the rest of her days . . .

The Reverend John Cotton didn't dare say anything good about the Separatists or even the Puritans from the altar of St. Botolph's, but by 1625 he had begun to simplify the ritual. He eliminated the large wooden cross at the ceremony of baptism. A few months later he said that from then on it would not be required for men and women taking Communion to kneel while receiving bread and wine. By 1627 he had succeeded in simplifying somewhat the elaborate robes of his calling. Anne Hutchinson noticed these things with the growing awareness that John Cotton was a full-fledged, ardent Puritan coming ever so cautiously out of his shell. She was apprehensive on hearing dissatisfied voices raised at his abandonment of long-respected ways. However, she noted too that there had begun to be some in the congregation, such as a Mr. Bartholomew, who dressed as plain as a pikestaff, who were of a puritanical bent themselves.

Anne found no fault with this newly emerging Cotton; after all, what mattered was the way in which he interpreted God's Word to her, that was the purpose of ministers. However, one day in early 1630, Anne, at home, opened her Bible to a particular page; and it seemed to her with terrible clarity that God's Spirit was speaking directly to her! The verse her gaze had fallen upon was: "Suffer the little children to come unto me." And suddenly she knew that not only one of her small daughters but both would be stricken with disease and die that very year.

The dreaded happened. Her premonitions served, somehow, to comfort the grieving mother. At least God had seen fit to prepare her in His mysterious way. And now that she thought about it, she remembered that some similar warning had occurred back in 1623 before her small son had died. Other memories now surfaced of crises no doubt averted by her having come upon some peculiarly appropriate portion of the Scriptures.

Walking in the churchyard after the latest small coffin had been lowered into the ground, Anne found herself between her husband and Reverend Cotton, and confided her "revelations." Mr. Cotton was very understanding. He repeated that the role of the minister was to do this interpreting of Scripture for his people, but that perhaps in time of great need, the Spirit speaks direct.

Encouraged, Anne said, "I feel that nothing important ever happens that it is not revealed to me beforehand."

From behind her she heard a gasp. Turning, she saw Mr. Bartholomew, another one of the mourners. He looked very shocked. Seeing this, the Reverend Cotton laughed and said to Bartholomew that "of course she would not find many ministers who would let her 'have' that."

That was the end of the incident. At the time, it did not seem significant, certainly not enough to figure in a courtroom some thirteen years in the future.

In April, 1630, came the first great Puritan migration from England. One thousand settlers in eleven ships. Among the voyagers was John Winthrop, member of a distinguished family and a friend of John Cotton's. Winthrop was heading up a group of stockholders that called themselves the Massachusetts Bay Company, and their charter deeded them land in the vicinity of Salem. Like the Separatists of Plymouth, the emphasis was on religion rather than trade. Because of this, Cotton invited John Winthrop to come recruiting for planters in Lincolnshire, his platform the pulpit at St. Botolph's. And in honor of the occasion of having a real Puritan raise his voice in the Established Church, Cotton did another renovating job, this time on the altar, that most sacred section of a house of God, removing a lot of carved and fluted wood and marble that he had always felt detracted from the simple act of communion. This time his parishioners left no doubt of their disapproval. What would Mr. Cotton leave them, naught but the splendor of his sermons? And inviting an avowed Puritan into the Church! If this came to the attention of the Star Chamber, they might all find themselves in danger!

Cotton placated some of them by saying that Winthrop

would sound very much like himself, which was true but hardly comforting to his now-agitated congregation.

Winthrop came, a serious man looking aware of his responsibilities. Speaking with a slight stammer, he began his recruitments with an imitation of the town crier—perhaps to get his courage up, as he was primarily a writer, not a speaker: "Oh yes! Oh yes! All ye the people of Christ who are now here oppressed, imprisoned, and scurrilously divided, gather yourselves together, your wives and little ones, and answer to your several names as you shall be shipped for His service to the Western World for planting the United Colonies of New-England, where you will attend the services of the King of Kings . . ." He ended with: "We are to be a new Church springing out of your own bowels."

This reference to bowels was prevalent in those days. John Cotton's own follow-up speech, acknowledging the "pangs of parting from one's friends and country" said these pangs, "bid fair to tie up the bowels in a true lover's-knot." These tender sympathies were followed by assurances of the safety of the voyage. "Judge all of you whether the poor New-England people be not the forerunners of Christ's army, whether the Lord has not sent this People to preach in this wilderness! Of a truth He is with us. Of one hundred ninety-eight ships already sent forth, but one has foundered. Of many attacks by pirates not a shot has murdered one of ours in Christ. He has sent fog in most cases to hide his flock."

If Cotton's congregation did not realize, before the coming of John Winthrop, that they were being led by a Puritan, they knew it now.

The first warning from the Star Chamber came soon after. "Cease and desist" was the gist of the command. "Upon pain of removal."

But it seemed to Anne Hutchinson that her minister was, like one of her children, running a fever.

*

The great day arrived, chilly but clear; the *Arbella* and several other ships of the Puritan fleet set sail from Boston to rendezvous with the others at Yarmouth; John Cotton and a few of the faithful of his flock, including Mr. Bartholomew and Anne, came to see them off. For the rest of Cotton's congregation, they begged him not to "draw attention to himself on this notorious occasion," as there would be officials of the Crown all over the place, checking visas, swearing passengers to allegiance to the king and checking lists for names of those people wanted for examination by the Star Chamber. But Anne Hutchinson could see that nothing could keep her Reverend Cotton from being in on the great embarking.

From the deck of the *Arbella* John Winthrop addressed his people: "We must consider that we shall be a city upon a hill! The eyes of all people are upon us, so that if we shall deal falsely with our God in this work we have undertaken, and so cause Him to withdraw His present help from us, we shall be made a story and a byword through the world!"

Applause, cheers, and shouts of goodwill from the assembled crowd. Then the ringing voice of the vicar of St. Botolph's carried across the water:

"Now all you people who are picked out by Christ to pass this Western Ocean for His honorable service—When your feet are once safely set upon the shores of America, be not daunted by your small number, for every common soldier in Christ's camp shall be as David, who slew the great Goliath, and his Davids shall be as the Angels of the Lord, who slew 185,000 in the Assyrian Army.

"You that are now shipped for this voyage, mind the work of Christ, and not some striving for titles of honor, others eying the best grass-plots and farms, for instead of casting down the enemies of Christ, this will keep you from striking one stroke in His cause. As for you who shall be promoted to highest places in His regiment, choose those beneath you with care, for although it may seem a mean thing to be a New-

England soldier, yet some of you shall have the battering down of the towers of those who can not be won by Christ. Then sound forth His silver trumpets, loud and shrill.

"The armies of Jehovah are at hand!"

The soldiers of the Court were at hand. They arrested the Reverend John Cotton in the name of the king and the Archbishop of Canterbury.

3

From Boston to Boston

A clothier's son had to work harder at being Archbishop
than the offspring of a peer. William Laud meant to go down
in history as having finally rid England of Puritans, Separatists,
Quakers, and the rest of that rabble who thought they could
worship any way they pleased. In the first year of Laud's
ascendancy, hundreds of ministers were called before him.
One of these was Anne Hutchinson's brother-in-law, an hon-
est, homely man in a wide-brimmed hat, whose mild-man-
nered sermons could hardly be heard to the back of his church
at Alford. Summoned, he was told there would be no ears
under that hat if he opened his mouth any more.

To Anne Hutchinson, it was happening all over again as it
had with her father. And now Laud was out to banish John
Cotton. Cotton stood before the Star Chamber and declared,
"I have not said in public I am a Puritan." That was the
crucial point in these cases.

He was told he might return to his pulpit if he mended his ways, and his altar. Put everything proper and aright again!

Cotton went back to St. Botolph's and nailed back a few wooden scrolls across the altarpiece. The following year, over babies squalling in the cold water of the baptismal font, he was again obliged to wave his wooden cross. Men and women receiving Communion were at various times on their knees, on their feet, and back on their knees again. Cotton was biding his time. As he said to his most loyal listener, Mistress Hutchinson, he had enjoyed some twenty years of good living in a wealthy parish and, although he had known for some time he would have to leave it, he'd like to wait until his friend Winthrop got the wilderness over there a little bit tamed.

It seemed sufficiently tamed in 1633 when Governor John Winthrop wrote Cotton that the colony had established a town. At first they had called it Three Mounts because of its modest hills. This was shortened to Tremont. And now, good Brother Cotton of Boston, England, they had renamed the town after your own; surely you will at least come and have a look at it?

Cotton would. Readying his family for the journey, he invited the Hutchinsons to come along. "You will be wheat fit for planting in the New World." Anne was thrown into an emotional turmoil, solved for the moment by two extenuating circumstances—she was eight months pregnant; and her twenty-one-year-old son Edward was begging to be allowed to go. The boy would be a link between herself and the beloved minister she might never set eyes on again.

The baby was a daughter, and baptized Susannah.
Early in 1634 a letter arrived from Cotton; all had arrived safely at this new "Boston," along with a son, born on board the ship and named Seaborn. "We did not baptize him on

board, not because of using salt-water, which is God's, but because a man-made ship did not seem like consecrated ground." The ship *Griffin* would return to England in a few weeks to pick up a shipment of cattle for the governor, and perhaps Mistress H. and family would glean some comfort about the safety of the voyage knowing it would be the same vessel that brought him and his so easily to these shores.

Anne sat in her bedroom with the door closed, and the family went quietly about the work, worrying about her.

She couldn't eat, she couldn't sleep. Here she was with a fine home, a loving husband, and eleven healthy children, and she felt she had lost everything, the light had gone out of her life. It was enough to make a woman feel guilty and wretched. Just because her pastor was gone from her, and there was no one now with whom she could spend a stimulating hour discussing some interpretation of Scripture! But Scripture was all there was for the mind to puzzle on. It seemed just not *fair* of God that her pastor, her teacher, should be taken from her. She wanted to follow him to America—but had she the right to ask her husband and family to pull up their own roots, to make the long dangerous journey, to start all over again in a strange and wild new land? Just so that she might continue to satisfy the craving of her restless mind?

In the 1930s a biographer of Anne Hutchinson wrote wondering whether she "loved religion in the form of her preacher, or loved her preacher under the guise of religion." It is still a question that probably no one can ever answer. All that is known is that Anne had a tremendous amount of energy that sought outlets—running a household and rearing a big family were just not enough. And, after a placid marriage of some twenty years spent in a quiet country town, no doubt she was at that stage of restlessness that preceded her girlhood move to London. She must have wanted to see more of the world before she settled down to old age, which came early in those days. And the increased, terrible activities of the Star Chamber were the talk of all England—the protestor William Prynne having been shorn of his ears, branded, and imprisoned for life for disapproving, among other things, the marriage of King Charles to a Catholic princess. Anne honestly feared for her country's future.

If only God would speak to her, as He had so often, through the pages of his Word, and give her a sign, then she would know what to do!

Shortly after this, she opened her Bible to the Book of Isaiah and her gaze fell on the verse: "Thy teachers shall not be removed in a corner any more, but thine eyes shall see thy teachers."

There, nothing could be clearer than that! (She forgot, like most people of a mystical bent, all the times she had looked in the Bible and had not discovered any personal relevance in the words.) Perhaps her family also had been waiting for a sign; at any event, they did not protest much when she spoke of her desire to go to America. Will Hutchinson was always eager to do whatever might keep his wife content.

It was a spring day in 1634. On that day Anne made the decision that was to cause more agitation and turbulence in New England than anything that had happened before.

> Could we with ink the Ocean fill
> Was the whole Earth of Parchment made
> Was every single stick A Quill
> Was every man A Scribe by Trade
> To write the Love of God alone
> Would drain the Ocean dry
> Nor wou'd the Scroll contain the Whole
> Though stretched from Sky to Sky!

A fine verse for chanting while on deck of the *Griffin*, flying over the calm of Atlantic swells, under a sunny blue sky. The little group from Lincolnshire didn't sing—singing was a pagan thing—but they chanted in jubilation. Behind them was the ordeal of being searched by the king's guards who had come aboard before the ship could sail, demanding the oath of allegiance to Britain, scrutinizing the passenger list for Star Chamber escapees, then grudgingly issuing passports. Now finally they were free, free to hold meetings, recite favorite psalms, and give thanks to the Lord!

With Anne and her husband and children was her sister Mary, whose husband, the "silenced" Reverend Wheelwright, was soon to follow them. And Anne was happy that her long-time friend Mary Dyer had also promised to follow them all to America as soon as her husband sold his millinery business. Will Hutchinson had brought his own business with him. The bolts of cloth he carried in the ship's hold cost four pounds a ton. And it was five pounds apiece to transport himself and his wife, with reductions for children according to age. He would have to work very hard in the new country to regain his former security, but his wife's cheerful manner, her revived good spirits, were infectious: Things were going to work out all right!

The trip took eight weeks; and, as Anne was later to write, it was not all blue skies. "Three thousand miles through ten thousand dangers," referred to two bad storms, sharks that followed the ship, and a pirate vessel that approached but apparently thought better in view of the *Griffin*'s guns. Also: "We spent the voyage in painful proximity to Winthrop's cattle,"—a hundred head the governor had ordered, most of them bellowing and seasick. Then there was the poor food—salt meat and fish, hard bread, oatmeal and beer, and nearly everybody had forgotten to bring along lemons or limes as had been advised, to help prevent scurvy. "Of two hundred of us only four were lost." Despite the dangers and discomforts, Anne was happy, every day bringing her closer to Boston and her spiritual friend. And yet, every day of that voyage she was unwittingly behaving in a manner that was making for her two implacable enemies.

Along with her high spirits went a physical restlessness at being obliged for long weeks to spend the time in the limited space of a small ship; and so she cast round in her mind for something to alleviate this. In the discussions on religion that were always going on, Anne began drawing to her a little group of women with the idea of further discussion from a woman's point of view. Soon this group began growing, and in a few weeks Anne found herself the teacher, or leader, of some fifty women, enthusiastic to learn of her interpretations and happy of the chance to voice their own points of view, which in the company of men they never had the chance of doing. This "new meeting" for women only was viewed with astonishment by most of the men on board. Women massing to themselves, airing their own ideas of the Holy Word—it was just unheard of. Especially surprised and incensed were two men of importance, the Reverend Zacharias Symmes and Mr. Bartholomew. This Bartholomew was the same man who had overheard Anne state, in the churchyard at Alford, that God spoke directly to her through the Bible, of revelation of events to come in her life. He now shared this information with the Reverend Symmes, who was profoundly shocked. The Almighty taking the time and trouble to talk to an individual human being, and not even a minister at that? What heresy! And could it be that this was the stuff Mistress Hutchinson was teaching that flock of females she had gathered about her? No wonder many of these women were bypassing *his* meetings to attend hers.

He had not long to wait to discover what Mistress Hutchinson was teaching the others. Every person had the ear of God if only she or he would ask for it, and listen to the answer. And Jesus had plucked corn on the Sabbath to show His contempt for man's laws governing conduct. Plucking corn to assuage one's hunger wasn't the same as working on the Lord's Day; in other words, you should interpret the Law as your own conscience dictated. This, said Symmes to his fellow passenger, Bartholomew, was anarchy.

In the heady atmosphere of an ocean voyage to a new land, with a group of listeners apparently as eager for good discussion as she herself had been, Anne waxed eloquent without the slightest worry as to how her ideas might be taken. And her family caught the spirit of her exultation. Will Hutchinson proudly announced that the Lord had revealed to his wife the very day of their safe arrival in America. And their oldest daughter, Faith, created a small commotion of her own; she had been given divine knowledge that a certain young man on board was doomed to an early death, but he would be saved if he "would walk in the ways of my mother." At this, the Reverend Symmes approached Faith's mother, who had her eight-months-old baby, Susannah, in her arms, and inquired politely if the child had babbled anything of "super-natural import," which might save them all. He wrote that Anne gave a "ready, practical and witty reply." Perhaps it was the wit that stung the most. To make things worse, the *Griffin* came in sight of land on the very day—September 18—Anne had predicted. As the passengers bustled about readying themselves for going ashore, Bartholomew and Symmes put heads together. Someone in the village of Boston, Massachusetts, should be warned of the possible trouble-making qualities of this Hutchinson woman.

The ship glided past wooded islands, on one of which a new fort was being built; and so on to the town at the mouth of the Charles River. Anne saw cabins and frame houses scattered among hilly pastures, a fair and prosperous-looking place. Her spirits rose as she stepped ashore, for she saw, coming down the cobbled street to meet the ship, the familiar short smiling figure of the Reverend John Cotton. And there too was Anne's son Edward, running to greet his parents and brothers and sisters. For the next hour or two Anne's cup of happiness ran over.

Later that day, when Anne and her family had been settled, more or less, in new quarters, Anne realized she had not had a chance to talk to her friend, the pastor for whose sake she had traveled thousands of miles. She sought him out—and his face no longer reflected his beaming welcome. Hesitantly, Anne spoke of her eagerness to become a member of her pastor's new church.

Cotton's expression grew evasive. There had been some disquieting reports as to her "conduct and opinions." Her husband would be admitted immediately, but, ah, there would be a period of inquisition into her own qualifications.

He went on, stammering a few more phrases. "Here it be tactful to hold one's tongue. . . . The state of affairs. . . . It will be for only a little while. . . ." Then he rallied. Of course she would be admitted to the congregation. Why, if anyone was not admitted, there would be no place for him in the community!

It was not the sort of welcome that Anne Hutchinson had envisioned.

4

More Terrible Than Imagined

Penelope Thomson, or Thompson, in 1634, was a pretty girl of twelve living in Holland's principal city, Amsterdam. Built about 1300 on wooden piles over soft ground, criss-crossed with canals and bridges, Amsterdam in the 1630s was a fortunate place to be growing up in—a city of bustle and beauty, teeming with Flemish merchants, Jewish diamond cutters from Spain and Portugal, and Huguenots—French Protestants—setting up leather-working and glass-blowing shops in their adopted country, where they had fled from religious persecution. To religion, Penelope gave scarcely a thought beyond Sunday services with her parents at the great New Church—Presbyterian—where, in the noisy, milling crowd, many a flirtation had its beginnings. The girl wore ribbons in her cap over yellow ringlets; her eyes sparkled; every day was an adventure. Something was always going on —a festival, an outdoor concert, a ship flying a foreign flag sailing right up to the street wall. And the city enjoyed an intellectual life perhaps second to none in Europe. The sciences of physics, astronomy, and biology were burgeoning alongside the arts. Not far from Penelope's home lived a young portrait painter, Rembrandt van Ryn, who was currently the rage of Amsterdam.

What was not going on under Penelope Thomson's nose was brought home to her by her tutor. Besides teaching her French and English, some mathematics and ancient history, he told her how proud she should be of her small country's history of expansion. The Dutch East India Company had driven the British and Portuguese out of Indonesia and Ceylon and won for itself the fabulous trade of the Spice Islands—which was the reason Penelope's mother cooked most foods with plenty of hot curries and chutneys—and the Dutch West India Company was now carrying on a thriving trade with the wild men, or "Indians," of the northeastern parts of America. It was said that despite their fierce manner and appearance one might barter quite easily with these creatures if one observed a strict policy of fair and open terms.

Recently the Dutch had conducted a successful barter for one of the Indians' islands, Manhattus; ships' captains returning to Amsterdam praised its wide, deep harbor, marveling that, unlike their own port, it remained ice-free the year round. A copy of a letter recounting the details of the purchase had been nailed up on the wharf (the only written evidence of the sale). From Deputy General Pieter Schaghen of Amsterdam to the States General at The Hague, it read:

5 November 1626

HIGH MIGHTY SIRS,

here arrived yesterday the ship The Arms of Amsterdam which sailed from New Netherland out of the Mauritius River [later Hudson] on Sept 23rd, they report that our people there are of good courage and live peaceably. Their women have also bourne children there, they have bought the island Manhattus from the wild men for the value of 60 guilders, it is 11,000 morgen in extend [22,000 acres], they sowed all their grain the middle of May, and harvested it the middle of August. Thereof being samples of summer grain, such as wheat, rye, barley, oats, buckwheat, canary seed, small beans and flax.

> 7246 beaver skins
> 178 ½ otter skins
> 675 otter
> 48 mink
> 36 wild cat
> 34 rat [muskrat]
> many logs of oak and nut-wood.

Other news spoke of ships sailing to the new settlement with their holds filled with flower bulbs; and one could see dismantled windmills, their great blades carried by sailors and deckhands, being loaded aboard America-bound boats. It must have seemed to a Hollander such as Penelope Thomson that this "New Netherland," far away as it was, must be a fair replica of her own familiar *Nederland*.

Except, perhaps, for those beforementioned "wild men"— although they did not seem so very wild, by the account of the Dutch who had dealt reasonably with them!

And so, by the time she was married, at twenty, Penelope must have carried in her mind a pleasantly colored picture of the Dutch settlement in the New World. At any event, when her young husband proposed that they leave Holland and set forth for New Netherland to see if they could make a home there, Penelope Thomson van Princes "went with willingness."

There is little on record of Kent van Princes, except that he was about his wife's age, and the two were married in Amsterdam in 1642. All that comes down to us of that time is Penelope herself, a woman blossoming into beauty, and with a cheerful and loving disposition. Had van Princes lived past his twentieth year there would probably have been more, in the records kept by Penelope and her descendants . . .

*

"On the forty-first day the cabin boy was washed overside."

It had been just before noon of a September day, but the sky was obscured, the wind a banshee sound, and the waves mountain gullies upon which the ship tossed, dipped, and barely managed each time to surmount, sliding again into the next gulf. The boy was not even heard to cry out; his head, a black speck, bobbed up once. A sailor on deck began to lash a line around his own waist, but then there was nothing but storm, and his crew mates urging him not to follow the lad to Davy Jones.

Penelope van Princes did not learn of the incident until a few hours later, and then she grieved for a while; the boy had been quick tongued and bright headed, and she had told her husband that she would like one someday just like him. But Penelope doubted that Kent had even heard her. Ever since they sailed he had been ill, and for the past week he had been delirious with fever; she had hardly emerged from their cabin, shared with half a dozen others.

The captain said they were all becoming weak from seasickness and he was fearful of scurvy, should they be blown off course and the voyage go on much longer. But young van Princes was worse off than the others, as if from some malady that had been working in him before the ship set sail. Along with her concern for her man, Penelope couldn't help feeling a bit sorry for herself. It just was not fair that she should arrive at this strange land—even if it was a replica of her own —without a strong, resourceful husband at her side!

On the fifty-eighth day, in the murky gloom of a stormy afternoon, the ship made landfall of a sort off a spit of land edged with rocky shoals. In fright and confusion the settlers shinnied down hand-burning lengths of rope into dories and rafts, some of which capsized in the heaving surf. Somehow Penelope, probably aided by sailors, managed to get her unconscious husband off the ship. It is not known whether the ship itself was broken up on the treacherous reach; but what is certain is that most of the passengers and crew managed to reach the shore. Now one can pick up the definite part of the history. Finding themselves on a barren expanse of beach, with dense woods looming behind this, the settlers held a short conference and decided to press on toward their destination, New Amsterdam, that very hour. Fear of the wild men decreed that no one spend a night on the unprotected beach. They urged the young Mistress van Princes to come along; it must be obvious even to her that her husband was about to depart this world. Penelope pleaded with them to help her carry Kent. Stern, pitying faces denied her; carrying van Princes would slow down the party on their way to the safety of the town. They left, promising to return as soon as possible with reinforcements.

Penelope was left on the beach with her husband, whom others had pronounced all but dead. The night came on; crouched beside Kent she slept fitfully. She must have known by then that she was going to have to face the New World as a widow.

But there are times when one's fears, great as they are, may be rendered pale by the onrush of reality. For in the morning came events more terrible than this pretty, sheltered young bride from Holland could possibly have imagined. In the morning, the wild men came.

She saw little—three or four men with feathers sticking up from shaved and coppery heads; then their arms were swinging down upon her with knives and with something she was to learn later was a tomahawk.

One blow of this weapon and the dying young man was dispatched. Penelope was deftly scalped; a knife slashed into her shoulder, and another stroke drove into and across her abdomen.

Then they left her for dead.

5

Scalped Yet Still in Certain Dangers

For what happened next one turns to Penelope's descendants, recounting her adventures of the year 1643. "She crawled to the edge of the wood . . . found dew in the hollow of leaves." "She ate fungous excrescences and the gum growing on trees." One can only imagine her physical and emotional pain. "On the fourth day she saw a deer run by with arrows stuck in its flanks, and she hid in a hollow tree. Then there came a dog racing across the beach, it stood barking at her and baring its rotted teeth till the wild men came up."

This time there were only two of them, one young, one older. The young one raised his tomahawk, but the older one stepped in front of him, frowning at the girl. In some versions of this part of the tale Penelope is said to have begged them to finish her off—as if they could have understood her; in others she simply cowered, whimpering, beside the body of her husband. What does agree, however, is the outcome: the older wild man apparently won the argument, because in an action that caused her mercifully to faint, "he threw his coat over her body and carried her off."

When she awoke, her first realization was that the terrible pain had disappeared. Slabs of a sort of mud had been applied to her bloody head. Her belly was wound tightly with cloth. Her mouth felt fuzzy, as if she had swallowed some drug; and for the moment she did not even feel panic that she was a young woman in a strange land, her husband butchered on its shores. The smell of cooking meat, fragrance of tobacco, domestic sounds of shouts, laughter, children's cries, and guttural arguments were enough to still fears for a while— Penelope let herself fall back into sleep, grateful just to be alive.

Waking, sleeping, a doubling of vision, times of screaming, glimpses of fierce dark faces hovering, rank smell of grease, nausea and vomiting, light as painful as splinters, blackness that terrified, a rough hand on her forehead, chills and consuming heat. And nightmares, of being chased by yelling wild men brandishing knives down an endless stretch of sand; and of being tied down in a hot, stifling enclosure—was she to be tortured?—and surrounded by the noise of people talking in a guttural tongue. She opened her eyes and saw far above her a peaked wooden ceiling; the shadow of flames flickered on the sides of what seemed to be a large hut; smells of cooking and women's voices were all around her. Was she awake or dreaming? Where was she? What had happened? Suddenly she realized she was being stared at; a little group of children, black-haired, copper-skinned and naked, was regarding her with the greatest interest.

Slowly, Penelope sat up. If this was another dream, at least it wasn't so bad as the others. Now she could see that she was in an oval-shaped enclosure with a floor of tamped-down earth and a fire blazing in the center; her pallet of straw was on a sort of low platform that extended around the walls. Across from her a few women were sitting, eating with their fingers out of small bowls. Penelope regarded them with more curiosity than fear. Their breasts were bare, their hips swathed in animal skins. Long, black, glossy hair was decorated with copper ornaments, shell beads, and pearls. And their faces were daubed with red paint, with black outlining the eyes. Penelope had a puzzled thought; what did that face decoration remind her of that struck her heart with a bittersweet pang? Yes, of Fêtes Day in Amsterdam, when everybody dressed as beggars, jesters, clowns. . . . Oh, how far was she from home?

Her self-pity turned fast into fear as two of the women got up and came over to her. But it was only to hold out a bowl of food. Penelope took it, and after hesitating, dug her fingers into the mushy contents, and began to eat. To her surprise the taste was delicious and she realized she was ravenously hungry. The swarthy women watched as she crammed the mush into her mouth and let it run down her arm, and then they began to laugh. They slapped their thighs with merriment; Penelope realized she didn't care. She was eating, she was out of pain, and for the moment not in any apparent danger. Suddenly she looked up to see a fearsome sight.

A wild man stood before her. His black hair was cut close to the side of his head, leaving a braided topknot streaked with gray, with bits of shells and stones tied in it; over this was a headband with a few feathers; a broad red line of paint curved down his forehead and across one cheek, and on his bare chest he wore strings of broken white and purple shells. For clothing there were a leather loincloth, stockings, and slippers. Penelope took in these details in an instant, then with a thrill of horror she thought, This was one of them on the beach. And she drew in her breath to scream.

But the wild man was addressing her. And somehow she was able to understand him! What was the language he spoke?

"I—save—you. I—chief. You—stay here." The memory of her tutoring came flooding back—he was speaking English! Penelope wanted to answer him in her gratitude that there was some miraculous means of communication, but after saying something peremptory in a guttural tongue to the women, he turned and strode away.

She must have come awake near nightfall, for soon the fire was banked and the little group made a few simple preparations for bed. Then all was dark and still, and Penelope closed her eyes once more. All of a sudden she remembered what had happened to her, and she put her hands to her head. And felt that she was completely bald. So that's what the women were laughing at. She cried herself, silently, to sleep.

Next morning she was awakened at daybreak, and soon was having her second experience in the New World, a cooking lesson. Afterward the woman—Penelope was later to learn the word squaw—took her outside. She discovered she was in a village of dome-shaped bark-covered shelters, with one near the center that was larger and longer. The squaw then took her through the surrounding woods and showed her a strip of beach, where she would be coming to fetch water and to pick clamshells.

Penelope looked across the blue waters of what seemed to be a bay, and saw another shore on which was a cluster of— houses! Smoke rose from several chimneys; these, thought Penelope, must be the homes of white settlers, perhaps those who had come over with her on the ship. If not, at least white skins, who would welcome her. And they seemed so near; but how to get to them?

As if reading her thoughts, the squaw "answered" Penelope quite clearly. She looked hard at the girl, then shook her head and drew a finger across her own throat.

Apparently the chief had given orders, she was to be kept in this place. But why, and for how long? Penelope was determined to get up the courage to ask him. But not that day; she didn't feel strong enough yet for a confrontation. And, besides, she was just the least bit intrigued at finding herself in such exotic surroundings.

Soon she was beginning to observe the people around her. "The men were tall, well-muscled, their faces fierce and noble. There was none among them lame, halt or decrepit." Winter had set in and snow was heavy on the ground. The wild men wrapped themselves in rough lengths of beaver and otter skins, and moved along the paths on wide-webbed foot coverings, the likes of which Penelope had never seen, but she could see they were right for staying on top of the snow.

She had been put to work breaking up clamshells, grinding the edges smooth with a stone, then threading the pieces through vines. She saw that the people wore these strings of shells as decorations, but soon she realized they used them also as barter. "They value the white parts of the shell much less than the thin purple rim. They weave belts of these bits, in designs depicting warriors throwing spears at heads of animals." She added that she must find out what these bits of shell were called. Perhaps she would use this question as an excuse to approach the old chief!

She did not have to approach him; he sent for her. And then she discovered why he intended to keep her in the camp. He wanted to practice his English!

The conversations that ensued must have sounded very odd —Penelope with her heavily Dutch-accented English, and "Tisquantum" with his guttural grunts—but they managed to communicate. He had, he said, been named for a noble ancestor, a "brave" who had been captured by the white skins that came in the big ships—captured by trickery, said the chief, black eyes blazing at his white-skinned listener. Years later this brave was returned to his homeland, and could by then speak the white skin's tongue, "the Yangees." (This was how Tisquantum pronounced "English.") And so when more of these people began to land on his shores he was able to converse with them, and even intercede for them with his chief, a great chief called Massasoit.

So now he, a lesser Tisquantum, but possessing his spirit with his name, had mingled with the white skins on these shores, learning something of their tongue but craving to know more, because it was helpful in barter so he would not be cheated, and in defending himself and his tribe from lies and unfair acts. Of which there had been very many!

Penelope wondered if the chief was speaking of that little group of "white skins" who lived in the houses she had seen across the bay; but somehow she did not dare ask. Instead, she asked him the name of his tribe. This seemed to please him greatly. The tribe was the Lenni Lenape, members of a great family all up and down the land, called the Al-gon-kin. There were other families, such as the Iro-quois, of which the Mohawks were their, the Lenni Lenapes', sworn enemies. But of course the Mohawks were not *men*. The only "true men" were the Lenni Lenape—this was the very meaning of the name! And so in event of personal insult, or in time of famine or war, it did not count, it was not bad, to kill them or torture them or eat them, as it would be to do to men.

Eat them! Penelope must have had difficulty concealing her horror. Her next question certainly changed the subject. What were the shells called that Tisquantum had hung about his neck?

"They are called wampum-peak," she noted, "and are used the way we use guilders [coins]. The names of the shelters are wig-wams, the meal-cakes I cook are sappaen, the parched corn from which they are made, ka-ha-ma-kun." She also noticed that the squaws had become quite polite to her since she had started conversing with their chief. "The word for thank-you is Wah-ne-sheh." "The squaws gave me a name, Wah-pay-wee-pit. I was told it meant the white-toothed one. The squaws' teeth are discolored and decayed. Will mine become so if I stay here?"

She must try to escape. Despite her strange new friend—and the implicit threat that he would have her throat cut if she did try to get away—she knew she must make the attempt. To do so a boat would be needed; Penelope would have to discover where the wild men kept the canoes she had seen them paddling on the water. She began lingering around the old warrior who was the official boat maker. She watched him hollow out a birchbark log with fire; controlling the flames with wet clay, he slowly reduced the interior to charcoal, then scraped it out with stone tools. When the boat was finished, Penelope exclaimed over its beauty; then she tried to be casual about following him and two other younger braves as they upturned the boat on their shoulders and marched it through the woods toward the beach. But the old man bringing up the rear shouted something at her and she lost her nerve and fled back to the camp.

A few days later, when she was again told to gather clamshells, she searched, heart in mouth for fear of being caught, the bushes at the edge of the wood, and came upon a canoe pushed up into a thicket. She promised herself, on the next moonless night . . .

Her desire to escape was given further impetus the next day when, to her fright and horror, she recognized the "other wild man," as she thought of him—the younger brave who had wanted to finish her off as she had huddled in the hollow tree. He appeared in the wigwam she shared with the "unattached" squaws, grinned at her evilly, and deposited a large gray-white fish at her feet. On seeing the fish, the squaws burst into shouts of laughter.

Mystified and alarmed, Penelope sought out the chief and was told that this was the same wild man who had scalped her and killed her husband. Since she had survived, he felt "possessive" toward her. He had brought her the fish, a type of salmon, for her to eat because it aroused sexual desire!

Penelope was horrified; but the chief added calmly that she need not accept the first brave who made such overtures; she might turn down two others. After that? It appeared clear to Penelope that after that there would be no more leeway allowed in choosing a mate.

She had been wearing a piece of fur around her shaven head; now she went around the village without it; this did not seem to make the least difference. Soon after the incident of the gray fish another young buck began loping along wherever she went. Number Two! She could not afford to wait for a moonless night; she would make a run for that hidden canoe the next time she found herself alone. But suddenly Number Two was, as it were, disqualified. It seemed that he had a wife, and had been unfaithful to her, and now the wife had the right to put him out of the village. The ceremony was attended by all. The braves clustered on one side of the clearing in front of the chief's wigwam, beside his "totem" pole; the squaws, children, and Penelope stood opposite. The young brave stood alone in the center of the clearing; his wife stepped up to him and in spite of the freezing weather, stripped off his outer garments, then his loincloth, after which she drew off his right leather slipper and left stocking. After that she gave him a hearty kick on the backside, occasioning laughter from the onlookers. And then the naked young man stalked off into the snowy woods.

Later Penelope asked the chief if he would not freeze or starve to death. No, he would just journey along the shore to another village of the Lenni Lenape, where all the single girls would vie for his favors. The same right to revenge was given a man if he caught his squaw in adultery, but he usually contented himself with giving her a public beating. Then Tisquantum was curious. Did Wah-pay-wee-pit feel pity? He had not known that whites had any of this quality. It was whites who had taught the "men" how to scalp, and had sent them out to kill the "non-men" of other tribes, paying according to the number of scalps brought back. Before the white skins brought knives, the men had only axes—stones

bound by thongs to wooden handles—and the club with gar-
fish teeth embedded in it. You could not scalp with these
weapons.

But he, Tisquantum, did not kill for its own enjoyment.
He, his tribe, his religion, respected life, all forms of life. You
paid homage to the animal you were about to kill, for in pro-
viding you with food, it was giving life to you. Standing
foursquare on a muddy path, Tisquantum divulged his phi-
losophy.

"We tell white skins, we willing to have a broad path for
you and us to walk in. If either asleep, pass by him, no harm
make, and no stump on path to hurt our feet. But if asleep, pass
by and do harm, then pact has been broken. We go on warpath."

Penelope asked about the religion of the Lenni Lenape. The
Great Spirit, said Tisquantum, was Manibus, who in the form
of a turtle supported the world on his back. Opposing him was
Hobbanock, the chief devil. Each year around this time, in
dead of winter, the tribe gave a festival in honor of Manibus
in hopes that he would cause the spring to come again. Tisquantum showed Penelope the face of the Spirit on the totem
outside his wigwam—totem being an Algonkin word for the
spirits of gods and ancestors that guarded a man's comings and
goings.

Penelope had pricked up her ears at the mention of this
festival approaching. If there was going to be revelry perhaps
she would have a chance to slip away!

The festival was held in the "longhouse" and lasted three
days. The chief wore a splendid outfit of burnished leather
and a vest made all of purple wampum-peak edged in white,
along with a huge feathered headdress; he sat on a platform
and heard grievances and requests from his people. A fan-
tastically masked medicine man danced before sick members
of the tribe. Penelope learned that the mask was the face of a
mythical forest creature that had the power to cure disease,

and indeed, many of the sick seemed better after being danced at. Other masks worn were of braided cornhusks to remind Manibus of the spring; when the corn was planted, these masks would be stuck on crossed poles in the fields, with coats flung over the poles; these would frighten the spirit of the cornfields, who would gather his birds and fly away. There was a lot of drinking of a bubbly amber liquid called beer-of-roots (to be sold in a later century as root beer) and smoking of tobacco—both Indian "firsts"—while the braves sat around playing a game using round rushes which they managed to shuffle and deal as though these were cards—and winning from one another all they possessed, a matter of shouting, groaning, and exchanging of wampum-peak strings and belts. And there were games of skill, such as one with half-shells of walnuts, one of which had a spot of red paint on it—Penelope likened this to a dice game. And to the beat of drums and chanting, the Indians danced, "two and two beside each other, or in three or four pairs," with the first pair carrying turtle or tortoise shells in honor of their god.

The first day, everybody kept going until morning, and there was no chance to escape. On the second night there was a full moon, and half the village was out in the clearing, masked and leaping in circles around a great fire. The young captive, watching from her wigwam, determined that come what may, the next night, the last of the festival, she would make a run for it.

By the following evening the participants were all either exhausted from lack of sleep or in a state of amorous drunkenness. Nobody seemed to be paying any attention to her. She slipped out of the longhouse and saw that the moon was obscured by clouds. It was now or never! She began walking in the direction of her tent, trying to appear casual. Suddenly rough hands seized her from behind and she was thrown to the ground. A young buck leaped upon her as her screams rang out.

A few squaws emerged from the longhouse and chased the fellow off—Penelope's potential Number Three. And then they led her back to the longhouse.

Spring, said Tisquantum, had arrived early that year. Manibus must have been pleased by his festival. The chief pointed out to Penelope signs of life—the quickening of small animals such as groundhogs, emerging from their hibernating burrows, looking like tiny bears; and overhead the strung-out V's of snow geese flying back from the south. And soon there came the busiest time of the year, in which everyone had a part except the chief—the drawing-off of the sap from maple trees. Penelope watched in fascination this strange way to get food—the Indians surely had not learned this from whites! The tree trunk was scored and a hollow wooden post driven in so that the sap could flow into a bucket. The day's run was taken into the camp where it was boiled until it became a thick, sweet syrup. The children of the camp made birchbark cones, filled them with snow, and flavored them with the delicious amber syrup. Penelope enjoyed this exotic treat—and must have been one of the first white women in the world to enjoy an "ice-cream cone."

Suddenly into this bustling, orderly scene came the angry mutterings of war. One of the men at work with the sugaring had looked up from his bucket just in time to see, or to think he saw, the headdress of a Mohawk disappearing behind a tree. He ran back to the camp with the news that their mortal enemies from across the small water were creeping up on them from all around. The woods were searched by every brave in the camp and there was not a Mohawk feather to be spied; but that night Tisquantum had a dream. In this dream the Mohawks raided the camp while everybody was busy with the sugaring and then set fire to the wigwams so that the very young children and old people were burned alive. A dream was a warning; the Lenapes would make war!

The next day the Indian chief was not the same Tisquantum practicing his "Yangeese" with Penelope. He recounted the dream with a face darkened with fury and fear. (Penelope learned later that when the Lenni Lenape dared take on any of the Mohawks, they ran the risk of half the Iroquois nation boiling down upon their heads—unlike the Lenape, who were less closely knit in time of trouble.) But dreams could never be ignored; always they were a warning from a friendly spirit; also, the dreamer had used up some of his energy, his life-force, in having the dream, and this he must recover by slaying the cause of it.

The sugaring was abandoned, the sap dripping into buckets until they overflowed, as the whole camp set to work getting ready for battle. The braves sharpened their spears and arrow-heads while the squaws prepared a cauldron of black paint for the decoration of the men's bodies. "They set the war kettle on the fire and danced around it, uttering yells more barbaric than before." Penelope was later told that this kettle was a sign that now the warriors were going out to devour their enemies, whether or not they actually ate them. The following day the chief emerged from his wigwam, dressed for battle; Penelope hardly recognized him in his fearsome decoration of black paint with blood-red streaks. He did not speak to her or to anybody else, but stalked off toward the wood, closely followed by one of the older squaws carrying two small bowls. Many, including Penelope, came along also, observing at a respectful distance.

Penelope knew where the chief was going—to his Living Tree Mask. This was the most important magic and was not propitiated except in time of war, to keep its magic potent. Only a chief could have one. Tisquantum's was a huge sawed-off trunk stripped of its bark; and the smooth wood had been carved into a likeness of the chief, with his mouth opened as if to receive food; then the face had been painted. The result was startlingly lifelike.

Tisquantum halted before his Tree and motioned to the squaw to give him one of the bowls. This contained cornmeal mush; he set it on top of the trunk. Then he reached for the second bowl, which held a little pile of shredded tobacco leaves; this he placed on the ground before the great face. Striking flint, he lighted the tobacco and blew upon it; as a thin stream of acrid smoke began to rise from the smouldering leaves, he took up the bowl of mush and with a bone spoon pushed some of the cereal into the open mouth. After that he gave the bowl and spoon back to the squaw and made a low obeisance, muttering phrases in his language. Then slowly he backed away from the Tree.

That evening at dusk they left, all the braves except very young boys and old men; the women went along with them down to the beach and watched their departure. The night was calm; the shadowy figures in the long canoes dipped paddles in the water in almost total silence and soon had disappeared from sight. Penelope wondered if the little band of people living in the "white" houses would be caught in the battle and be wiped out, leaving her with no place to escape to. At any event, until the wild men returned she would not have a canoe to escape *in*. The prospect was getting more discouraging.

By noon the next day they were back, dragging captives, and carrying three or four of their dead. While mounds were being dug for the slain Lenapes, the trussed-up Mohawks were tied to stakes, and spat upon and kicked by everyone, the squaws tormenting them most of all. Penelope crouched in the wigwam, trembling with apprehension. When the mounds of earth had been thrown up, the dead were buried in them; then the pent-up fury of the bereaved boiled over— and real torture began.

From the beginning Penelope could see, in the unabating savagery, the victim never doubted the outcome—and so helped his victors devise more and finer methods of burning and slicing, gouging and maiming. And never did the tortured warrior let out so much as a cry, even when he saw some of his own flesh, uncooked, being eaten. . . . At the height of the horror, Penelope sprang up from the floor of the tent and fled. No one leaped after her. All were too caught up in the hideous fun.

She ran pell-mell through the woods, stumbling, falling, scrambling to her feet. If she could not find a canoe she would throw herself into the water and swim until she reached land or drowned.

But she found a boat, carelessly left near the water's edge. Even so, she was unable to budge it an inch, though she pulled, pushed, and strained until her hands were bruised and bleeding. As the girl peered frantically behind her into the woods, the incoming tide lapped with maddening slowness under the keel of the boat. Finally it lifted, and she scrambled over the side.

It was a longer way than she had imagined. Hours seemed to have passed; dusk came on and the tiny houses seemed to grow no larger. One by one, then, their lights went on—they were beacons of encouragement to the fevered girl. As she lifted the heavy paddle from side to side her left shoulder, its muscles severed by the Indian's knife, gave her such agony that she lost consciousness briefly from time to time.

Finally, the little squares of lighted windows were drawing nearer. Penelope paddled with the wild energy that comes of desperation.

The canoe turned over.

She sank under immediately, so weak was she; then instinct took over and she struggled to the surface, thrashing about and swallowing water. Then the realization came over her that her feet were touching ground.

6

Stars on the Ceiling, Gold Coins in the Lining

Lady Deborah had just blown out the rush lamp in her son Sir-Harry's room when she heard the commotion outside. There were shouts, then the sound of pounding feet going past the house toward the beach. Lady Deborah hurried through the living room, drawing her dressing gown around her tall, spare figure. Oh, no, not those unfriendly Indians from the Long Island again! At this rate the community would never be finished! As it was now, her own house was the only one completed. Last week, some savages had thrown a burning brand into the stockade and the pigs and wild turkeys had all got away because the palisade wasn't yet completed—because the savages had stolen the fence posts.

Now she could hear the voices of her women neighbors as, with curiosity no doubt conquering caution, they were opening their doors. Lady Deborah was just as curious, and as the head of the community, felt responsible as well, and so she opened the top half of her door, built in imitation of the Dutch, as it let in air and kept out the livestock. The night was as black as—black velvet, the stars as thick as—the diamonds in Queen Elizabeth's crown, now on display in the Tower of London, where she would never view it again. *Damme, damme,* she swore like her late husband, how she missed that so-far-away, beloved, but infuriating country of her birth! And then she forgot her homesickness, for coming up the path were two of the young men guards in her employ, supporting what seemed to be a half-drowned boy. Lady Deborah fumbled hastily at the bottom latch. Into the parlor with him then, onto her Turkey carpet and yellow velvet couch, never mind, let's see what you have fished up and thank God it isn't Indians!

The next moment it was apparent, under the light of the table candelabra, that what they had was a young woman with hardly any clothes on and hardly any *hair*, just a little yellow fuzz. Lady Deborah gestured to one of the guards to put his jacket around the shivering shoulders. Then she knelt before the castaway and gently began to question.

The girl's first words were unintelligible. "Wah-nee-sheh, wah-nee-sheh!" Lady Deborah was at a loss. Then one of the guards said it sounded like the local In-jin dialect, something like "yes," or "thank you." Indian! But this child was no Indian. Good heavens, she must be a captive, escaped!

The curious neighbors were peering in at the door. Impatiently, Lady Deborah beckoned them to come in. The next hour was spent in getting the girl out of a fit of mild hysterics and into something clean and warm. She could not eat, and vomited even hot clear broth. She was put to bed, on a hemp-webbed cot next to Sir-Harry's bed; he awoke and stared, then went right back to sleep. Sixteen-year-olds with Indian friends and wolf cubs for pets took everything in their stride; and tomorrow that cub must go, or its dam would surely be around . . .

Lady Deborah sighed and softly closed the door. She would have a cup of her own good broth, sitting in her modern kitchen in the midst of a wilderness; maybe the steaming contents of the cup would clear her brain, as she asked herself, Why did she, how could she, still miss un-Merrie England?

She could have better understood missing France, say, where there was beginning to be an appreciation of elegance, and where scientist-musician-philosopher Descartes had devised a new method called geometry, and was advancing the refreshing idea that one should seek logical answers to the universe through a skepticism of illogical ones. In England they were still wrangling over how many angels could dance on the head of a pin. . . . Or Belgium, where, a full century before, the anatomist Vesalius had demonstrated that men and women have the same number of ribs: in England in those enlightened 1600s this was still heresy—for did not the Bible state in Genesis that God took a rib from sleeping Adam to create the woman Eve? And although to prove such anatomical details, Holland, among others, was permitting the dissection of corpses (and praising such acts when depicted by their leading painter, Rembrandt van Ryn), in England dissecting was still a hanging-and-quartering offense . . . and she doubted if the unimaginative English would see the irony in *that*. Ah, yes, and in Germany, following in the steps of the Dane Tycho Brahe, the Pole Copernicus, and the Italian Galileo, Johannes Kepler had come out with the belief that all the planets including the earth revolved around the sun; in England the earth, by royal edict, was stuck firmly in the center of Creation. Inspired by Kepler's idea of orbiting or circulating bodies, William Harvey, at the court of his monarch, James, had been proving that the body's blood circulates, instead of oscillating, or sloshing around, under the skin, a belief held sacred since the time of the ancient Greeks; court physician or no, Harvey was reminded that another scientist, Michael Servetus, for insisting on "circulation of the blood," had been burned at the stake by that Presbyterian defender of the *status quo,* John Calvin.

In Servetus's Spain, the court of Philip IV supported the sensual outpouring of the painter Velásquez; in Italy they had built Claudio Monteverdi a gilded house to mount his operas celebrating the pleasures of worldly love; and in England? William Byrd and Thomas Tallis, those good gray hammerers-out of hymn tunes given the exclusive right in all the realm to publish, and having died, nobody had been invited to take their place. Oh, but England did have a resident poet—about to make Italy his new home. John Milton had intended to make the Church his calling, but was now turning out pamphlets denouncing the rigidity of worship in, the impossibility of living one more year in—England!

Well, thought Lady Deborah, enough of these maunderings; what mattered this year was action. This was the new England, and in it she was building a town. A favor had been granted her by men who had never heard of a woman's concerning herself with real estate, but they were respectful of her money; and now she was being constantly threatened by maverick savages who tried to steal or burn down everything she managed to put up. Yes, action, progress. . . . Tomorrow she would exhort the men to work harder on finishing the building of the houses and stockade, perhaps by an extra ration of rum—sailors or carpenters, Englishmen all had a common thirst. And she would inquire into the story of that poor waif deposited tonight upon her door-stoop. . . . What a strange life it was turning out to be. Still, better than being sentenced to, and then forgotten in, some dank dungeon known only to God—and the Star Chamber.

She had been born Deborah Dunch in 1600, her father, Walter, a member of Parliament in Elizabeth's reign. Sir Walter brought to his daughter a sense of natural privilege, the right to education and travel and to the speaking of one's mind. Although as a woman she could not attend Oxford or

Cambridge, up until her marriage she had the best tutors available and attended the Sorbonne in Paris. At twenty-two she married Henry Moody of Garsden, Wiltshire, the year he was created a baronet by King James. The next decade was spent on Sir Henry's estate as Deborah supervised the laying out of flower and vegetable gardens, and redesigned the wings of the mansion to include such novelties as a "greenshouse." In summer the king often received at Gravesend, a watering place at the mouth of the Thames River where it emptied into the North Sea. One distinction of the place was that, a few years before, an Indian "princess" had died there and was laid to rest in a grassy plot of the parish church, near the river's landing stage. Her name was Pocahontas, meaning "the playful one," and she had saved the life of the English captain John Smith when he was threatened by her father, an Algonkin chief, in Virginia of the New World. Pocahontas had married another Englishman, John Rolfe (or Wrolfe), and sailed with him across the Atlantic; in London she had been presented at the palace to James and his queen as a regal and comely princess; then, on her way home, she had been stricken with a fever; the ship put in at Gravesend, where Pocahontas succumbed. Her headstone read that she was just twenty-two years old. This was Lady Deborah's first "encounter" with American Indians, and it left her with a sense of the romantic that she was later, to say the least, to lose.

After only ten years of marriage, Sir Henry died of a stroke, leaving his widow with a five-year-old son. (A daughter, name unknown, had died in infancy.) The son, having inherited at birth his title of baronet, now became known with affection as little Sir-Harry. Deborah spent the next four or five years working in her gardens and giving small concerts for friends on the harpsichord. Becoming increasingly restless in this narrow tradition of rural society in which her marriage had placed her, she finally wrote to the Star Chamber, England's dread court-without-appeal—with its deceptively beautiful stars painted on the ceiling—for permission to travel.

What she had in mind was taking herself and the boy off to Paris, Berlin, or Vienna; what she was given, after months of humiliating pleading, was a paper permitting her to journey the eighty miles to London! At the same time the Chamber suggested she stay at home and manage her lands so that they might earn the largest possible tithe—the 10 percent tax due the Established Church on all profits emanating from an estate.

Well, if she could not go farther than London, at least she would stay as long as she liked. Her visits grew longer and longer until she was daring the thought of closing down the estate and going to live in the city. She saw Shakespeare's *King Lear;* she met Ben Jonson in the last year of his life—the two discussed Jonson's first trade, bricklaying, a skill to figure in Deborah's future. And she was attending secret religious meetings of the Quaker and Baptist sects, at which stimulating ideas were discussed. The Star Chamber wrote a stern warning; they had been informed of her attending meetings of these illicit societies, and now forbade her any further travel at all, on pain of losing her estate to the Crown. *Signed:* Laud, Archbishop of Canterbury.

Lady Deborah's aristocratic hackles rose; this son of a clothier dared to curtail her freedom of movement and threaten her with the poorhouse to boot! She replied with a note that verbally rapped knuckles, and set off with Sir-Harry on a grand tour of the country, counting on her importance to get them past county border guards without papers. Sir-Harry should be shown his rightful heritage—Roman walls and baths, medieval castles and the site of the Magna Carta, that four-hundred-year-old guarantee of every Englishman's right to spiritual and physical freedom.

They were arrested at the borders of Wiltshire and escorted home under guard, where notice was served that in spite of her title, lands, and wealth, she was summoned to appear within the week before the judges of the secret court.

Now she knew she must indeed let go her lands if she hoped to escape with her life. Where to flee? France came first to mind; recently England's only philosopher, Thomas Hobbes, had managed to reach Paris after having fallen into dangerous disfavor with the Church because of his earthly emphasis on the life of man—"solitary, poor, nasty, brutish and short." However, friends informed her, Hobbes was already in trouble with the great number of Englishmen who had settled in France, bringing their Puritan beliefs along. Hobbes's predicament made one thing suddenly clear to Deborah. She had had enough of the stultifying atmosphere of ancient customs preserved at the expense of good minds. What was wanted was not Old Europe but the New World, where surely the winds of personal freedom would blow.

On a spring day in 1640, at the port of Bournemouth, Lady Deborah and thirteen-year-old Sir-Harry were among other passengers trudging up the gangplank of a ship bound for Boston, America. But these two seemed to be trudging with more difficulty than the rest; although each carried only one small valise containing nightclothes, they were having difficulty standing up straight. Examining bags and papers at the ship's rail was an official of the Crown; when Lady Deborah presented her belongings she was waved aboard with only a perfunctory search.

The official, like all the others it had taken to get them this far, had been liberally bribed. Still, Lady Deborah observed later, "I was glad no one thought to have us weighed."

Sewn into the lining of their clothing were hundreds of gold coins, each wrapped in cloth to reduce the danger of a telltale *chink*. They spent the two months' voyage in these clothes, fearful of being robbed and murdered.

Boston in 1640 was a cluster of humble houses, but no immigrant ever arrived on her shores who found the sight more beautiful.

7

"A Pie-Shaped Wedge"

A week later Lady Deborah was owner of one of the few Boston houses of quarried stone, thus a landowner in the Territory of New Netherland, the name for the entire tract from "Main" south to the island on which stood the town of New Amsterdam, its capital. She was also received by the governor of Massachusetts.

Governor Winthrop seemed to his visitor to be the epitome of an English gentleman of culture, a type whom she had held out faint hopes of meeting on this side of the ocean. And so, over an excellent tea, she relaxed, speaking freely of her reasons for leaving England. Why, she did not even attend that Church she'd been forced to pay tithe to, being more in sympathy with the Baptists. . . .

The governor's genial manner changed. Did that mean that her son was not baptized? Yes, was Deborah's reply. She believed children should not undergo important ceremonies until they were old enough to understand them.

But, said the governor, did she not realize that if the boy were to die this very day, he would go straight to Hell? And . . . had she not said she had lost another child in infancy? Was that child, too, unbaptized? Of course, said Lady Deborah.

In the diary of Governor Winthrop he writes of "Ladye Moodye, a very wise and anciently religious woman, but with erroneous views on religious matters." The actual meeting may have ended on a less restrained note, for Lady Deborah's reply to his inference of her daughter's eternal damnation was, "What kind of God do you imagine?"

It took her less than a year to realize she couldn't settle down in Boston for the rest of her life. And from the beginning people had been coming to her, speaking of their own dissatisfactions with the concept of religious freedom as observed by the Massachusetts Bay Colony. They spoke of the banishment of several people, including the preacher Roger Williams for, among other things, his disapproval of infant baptism. They also spoke of hearing about greater freedom of religious worship in the "sister" colony at Salem.

Well, said Deborah, since they were all of one mind, why not see about chartering a boat, and sailing up to Salem? Everyone was in enthusiastic agreement. And Lady Deborah considered it a good omen that the name "Salem" was a Christianized corruption of *Shalom*, the Hebrew word for peace.

The first sight that registered on the little party disembarking was the stock. A woman sat in this wooden contraption, her legs stuck through holes in the boards. Her head was lowered as if in shame.

The moment Lady Deborah met the minister of the Salem church she expostulated. The minister assured her the woman was not being punished for a strictly religious offense; some young girl had claimed to have seen her practice witchcraft;

the woman had confessed to being temporarily possessed of the Devil; she was now being made an example of. It was nothing; and he would be proud if this great English lady would take up her abode in the colony. Lady Deborah again tried to make a home for herself and Sir-Harry; although she had lost money on the quick sale of her Boston house, she now bought a four-hundred-acre farm in nearby Swampscott, "paying quitrent to Master Humphries, 1100 pounds." She was soon also to lose out on this transaction. As a condition of living in the colony she had been obliged to join the church, and now everybody was after her, just as back in Boston, to have Sir-Harry baptized!

A woman not passionately concerned with religious matters, liking above all peace of mind, comfort, and simple pleasures, Lady Deborah would probably have given in at that time and permitted her big son to be dunked piecemeal in a marble font built for babies. But the insistence of the people of Salem that if she did not perform this, to her, purely symbolic act her son was in danger of hellfire, "got her back up," just as had the Archbishop of Canterbury.

The next thing she discovered about Salem, to her dismay, was that the colony was engaged in a thriving slave business—captured Pequot Indians were exchanged for Negroes from the West Indies island of Barbados who were deemed bigger and brawnier than the usually fine-boned Indians. When indignantly inquiring about this practice, she was told by a minister, "But this has always been done. These slaves have been taken in their battles with other blacks, and these blacks sell them to us!" Lady Deborah had half realized the fact of slavery back in England; here it was out in the open, and not even the most pious worthy thought twice about it. After all, Negro or Indian, neither was a Christian and so was not a *person*. To the Salemites, it mattered far more whether her son was baptized!

In a matter of months she was facing the threat of excommunication. She would not put up with such an indignity; she would leave of her own free will. The farm at Swampscott had cost her dear. Her shrinking fortune meant that next time she bought she would have to make sure. But where in this land of transplanted Englishmen was she to find any less intolerance than there was back in England?

In desperation she considered the Dutch down in New Amsterdam. Maybe Hollanders would be a cut above her freedom-denying countrymen. But this time she wouldn't buy more land for a year.

She bought within weeks!

On a clear morning in 1642 she had been rowed ashore from the North (later, Hudson) River to New Amsterdam, there greeted by Nicholas Stillwell, agent of the Dutch West India Company, the man who had been given the right to deed plots in the Dutch area of Bruijkleen (*Broik-leen:* later, Brooklyn). Stillwell had already assured her that in the New Amsterdam area there was true religious freedom; it could not be otherwise, for here were living such different peoples as Danes, Norwegians, Portuguese Jews from Brazil, Bohemians from Slavic lands, as well as the Dutch and some English, to say nothing of those others who weren't expected to have any religion—Indians, African slaves, and pirates from Spain. And he had offered to prove this with a guided tour of the town.

"Welcome to a European outpost of culture in the New World," were his opening words to Lady Deborah, and taking her arm, he guided her up the wide riverbank that was called the Beaver's Path. This led them past a windmill which, to Lady Deborah pausing beneath it, looked as high as the masts of a ship. Stillwell said the Beaver's Path was called Dirty Street by the townspeople, and she could see why: flour from the mill had sifted over everything, and cattle grazed beneath the great sails. Before she had even turned from Dirty Street into Heere Street (later to be called Broadway by the

English), she had proof of Stillwell's claims: there were women and children whose complexions ranged from Scandinavian to Mediterranean; Indians hurrying by, intent on the barter of an armload of furs; sailors; merchants on horseback; a short line of Negro slaves in chains (Stillwell said they would mainly be sold to the Virginia planters, to pick in the fields for the burgeoning tobacco industry) and, withal, she could make out a comforting phrase in English now and then.

In the open space at the beginning of Heere Street a cattle market was doing brisk business. Across the road a group of men in uniforms was being put through marching paces by a fife-and-drum duo; Stillwell said they were the soldier-guards attached to the fort. This stronghold was built in the shape of a four-pointed star. Beyond it the street was lined with houses recalling their Dutch homeland, with red tiled roofs, stepped gables, and gardens colorful with flowers and spring vegetables; Lady Deborah lingered as she passed those houses. Stillwell said that many of the houses belonged to the people who kept the town abuilding—ships' carpenters, surveyors, chairmakers, coopers (barrelmakers), and the midwife, whose importance in a community of less than five hundred could not be overestimated. Also, members of the West India Company lived in this row—there, across the way, was his own house; the company agent invited Lady Deborah in to meet his family. Mrs. Stillwell bustled up, drying hands on her apron and shooing the children outside. She showed Lady Deborah around their simple abode. The one large room revolved around the fireplace, heart of the house. Beds were built into the walls, with drawers beneath that pulled out for children to sleep in. A half-floor above, reached by a ladder, made room for extra beds and storage. Stillwell said there had been talk of taxing a house by the number of floors, and this half-floor was the colonist's way of having his cake and eating it. Colonists had to be continually on their toes to outwit even the most benign of mother countries! Mrs. Stillwell

served a plate of warm scones with butter from her own cows
—and fresh coffee, a beverage Lady Deborah once said she
could not function without for three hours running. Re-
freshed, she and Stillwell continued on their short round trip.
Beyond a branch of the Main Canal was the poorhouse, where
the poor, aged, and orphans were cared for. (These were
mainly Dutch, Stillwell observed; but who had to chip in
with taxes to feed them? She guessed it: the English. Lady
Deborah could see there was a certain amount of friction between Dutch and English in this small but burgeoning community.)

Next they passed the Marketfield, a sort of common, across
which could be seen the main canal, which provided access
to the market area and mooring for small fishing and trading
boats. Stillwell guided his guest across the Brewer's Bridge;
Lady Moody pronounced the area dirty, smelly, and practical.
Across the bridge was a tavern that served also as the town
jail, which, said Stillwell, they were planning to turn into a
city hall—his attitude implying the *English* would never build
their city hall out of a tavern and a jail! And here were five
attached houses of the West India Company where Lady
Deborah might buy a great many things without having to
send to Europe for them. Now they began on their return
journey, looking across the Marketfield toward "the Long
Island," across the East River, anchorage for the company's
seagoing vessels. These carried beaver skins, lumber, and salt
fish for Amsterdam; they would return with tools, seeds,
household goods, and other necessities for the settlers. Past the
Weigh House for these goods stood the town gallows, though
they were seldom used; convicted murderers were sent back
to Holland or England for punishment. On the beach near
a pier and the Weigh House was the marketplace. Here
farmers brought beef, pork, butter, cheese, turnips, carrots,
and other produce to sell "on the beach." The market was on
Pearl Street, so named for the many oyster shells left there by

early Indian encampments. At the foot of Pearl Street a ferry plied its way to and from Bruijkleen mornings and after-noons, "except," said Stillwell, "in tempest weather, when the windmill has taken in its sails." There was as yet no ferryboat man; the first person aboard took the tiller, the results being, said her guide, many a near-capsizing. Past the ferry slip one could see the city wall, a wooden stockade upon which it was hoped that soon guns could be mounted. Beyond the wall was the bouwerie, or farm, of Director General Kieft.

Back again at the end of the island, women were spreading freshly laundered linens out to dry on the grassy plot that served as the common bleaching ground. Lady Deborah stopped to see if any of the women spoke English. Three or four of them did; and as Stillwell waited, indulgently, one was telling Lady Deborah of how a dog had run off with a pillowcase last month, and the dog's owner had been sued, as if it had been trained to steal the neighbor's linen! Lady Deborah resumed her walk with a feeling of camaraderie with these women, seeming so free to chuckle over a bit of gossip. By now she was "of a mind" to consider buying land near such neighbors.

But—where was their church? Oh, said Stillwell, almost as an afterthought, at the top of the hay barracks! He pointed to a large wooden building nearby, where he said the hay from the fodder boats was stored. A spacious room had been built above this area, where the people could congregate on Sundays and listen to the Bible being read by a series of Dutch and English preachers; above this room, Stillwell pointed out, was the tower in which a bell had been hung; this bell was from Dutch booty captured from a raid on Puerto Rico in 1625. "And that is the weather," said Stillwell, "in which we worship in New Amsterdam."

Fair weather, indeed! In answer to her questions as to the terms of a plot in Bruijkleen—the name meaning "Free Loan" —Stillwell said that settlers must pay to the company a tithe of all things grown on the land for ten years, after which the property was "theirs forever." Now, that was a tithe Lady Deborah thought she could respect! But, added Stillwell, there was a fly in the ointment, and its name was Willem Kieft. All purchasers of Dutch plots had to sign a contract with the general, and he was not altogether to be trusted. Back in Holland he had been charged with embezzling the ransom entrusted to him to rescue Christian captives held by the Turks, had had his picture stuck up on the gallows, and had fled to America to escape debtors' prison or worse. But to be fair, last year Kieft had signed a treaty with one Jonas Bronck for lands to the north (later to be known as The Bronx), and all seemed aboveboard; still, one must remember, this was Kieft dealing with a fellow Dutchman. At the moment the general was harassing the English fur trappers, demanding a share in every pelt, and attempting to tax the Indians to help maintain the protection of the fort, when its soldiers offered no protection for them. How did Kieft consider Indians? He had set the ferryboat charges: "For a Wagon and two Horses, 20 Stuyvers, for an Indian, 6 Stuyvers, for a Person, 3 Stuyvers." Because of Kieft's "chivvying trickery with Indians," just the year before, said Stillwell, he himself had lost his tobacco plantation in New Amsterdam and had been forced to flee for his life.

All this made Lady Deborah curious to see this arch-villain of a general. She accepted Stillwell's invitation to stay overnight and visit Kieft at the fort next morning.

"A pie-shaped wedge, set at the mouth of the Narrows, with a good deep harbor of its own, with the ocean on one side and the village of New Amsterdam on the other." That was the description of the "Bruijkleen" land that Lady Deborah, together with the group that had come down with her from Salem, had just signed a patent for. Director General Kieft was most generous in his outlook; perhaps in time this pie-shaped wedge with its fine harbor would give New Amsterdam itself a run for the shipping money!

Deborah's reaction to the general had not been unfavorable; after Archbishop Laud, back in London, perhaps all other villains were minor ones; and she had been instantly taken with the land she was offered. But Nicholas Stillwell had demurred over her quick decision. The director general had not seen fit, had he, to mention the fierce Mohawk Indians roaming the adjoining Long Island. Well, yes, allowed Kieft, but they had been put down thoroughly last year, had been found to possess no firearms or "firewater"; and he assured Lady Moody that he would personally send over some of his best soldiers to guard the area while she was in the process of building.

And so it was that Lady Deborah Moody was granted a patent to lands for the purpose of erecting a town upon them in the year 1643—the first woman in America to be given this privilege. But the patent was "provisional"—it would be made firm in a year or so, as soon as "any claims by the aborigines that might come up were settled." The aborigines, Kieft's term for Indians, were always claiming that the land the white man settled was theirs, which was nonsense, since they weren't living or farming on it!

Lady Deborah was so buoyed at the prospect of building a town to her own specifications that she swept all doubt aside. A town in which she and others might live "in absolute freedom of conscience, with representatives chosen by all the people." If she could make this ideal come true, all that had gone before would be worth it.

Meanwhile, she restored Stillwell's good humor by investing most of the money she had left in Dutch West India stock. Stillwell assured her she was helping to build the new America; Lady Deborah was thinking more of having the means of settling a dowry on Sir-Harry when he married. She was lucky; the company burgeoned in exploration and trade from the Caribbean to the fur-rich forests of Quebec. As she wrote to friends in England in the ensuing years, there was a "romance" in lending money toward the development of a whole new continent. And every handful of gold coins delivered to her came with a story to it!

The plans for the town and their execution proceeded with everybody's enthusiasm sky high. Lady Deborah laid out the town with a square in the center comprising about sixteen acres, which would be enclosed by a palisade fence for protection against Indians and wolves. Forty triangular lots would radiate outward from the square for a few rods (a rod being 5.5 yards), their apexes resting on the town fence. Thus each owner could leave his house and farm his acreage without trespassing even a foot on his neighbor's land; and each might swiftly retire within the palisade to take up common defense. Every night the cattle would be herded inside the square, wherein would be the church, school, town hall, and burial ground. And each house would have its own "ha-ha," a wall set low about the garden so as not to obstruct the view.

And what to call her town? Lady Deborah thought of the happiest times of her life, on holidays and state occasions with her husband, in another town situated at the mouth of a river where it emptied into the sea. There was only one name for this town. Gravesend.

The people of Gravesend were building. The neighboring Indians were watching, silent and curious. And the director general was paying weekly visits, advising.

If Lady Moody would forgive his saying so, it was quite chancy of her to let the aborigines stand around so freely; they were obviously planning to steal the horses. Aborigines, said the general, over the tea that Lady Deborah could not help offering him, though she dearly wanted to get on with the whitewashing of her kitchen, never had horses until the white man came, and now they are so wild about them they will risk their lives to steal them. Aborigines are at the lowest state of civilization; they have not yet learned more than the rudiments of agriculture, and that was developed by their squaws; they are nomads and have never learned the value of keeping and raising animals. They had no metal for knives or silver for ornaments until the whites came along because they never learned how to get it out of the ground. They never learned how to distill alcohol; they have no written languages, and from tribe to tribe, even within the same area, if they meet they can scarcely understand one another. And in all the thousands of years they must have been in America they had not even invented the wheel!

To this Lady Deborah observed that the *Indians* had invented the hoe, that they had taught the white man how to plant corn, and how to tap trees for maple syrup; and she believed that if they were treated with fairness and decency they would respond in kind. For instance, she had put up, in sign language, a promise of a bounty of five guilders for the killing of each wolf, and at least two Indians had brought her wolf carcasses, received their pay, and departed peaceably.

Kieft appeared not even to hear. The aborigines should never be given alcohol. There were wild apple trees in Gravesend; these should be cut down, because the fermented juices of the fruit made birds giddy and drunk, and even the dumb aborigines might catch onto this, too.

Lady Deborah's patience was stretched; but she remained polite. And did not cut down her apple trees! Mainly she was happy building her new life. The furniture, rugs, and other household items she'd ordered from England had arrived, and she and Sir-Harry had a home again. The sights out her kitchen window were sometimes reminiscent of England, and at other times not at all. For instance, the fodder boats: the first time she had seen one she could hardly believe her eyes. A beamy little craft, it was filled from deck to masthead with an enormous block of fresh green hay; the boat's stays had been fastened through the bale, and a sailor was perched like a doll on top. Her inquiries revealed that the fodder boats carried hay from "Staatan" Island to the dozens of livery stables in New Amsterdam, where land was too precious to be wasted on fields of hay. Then there were the herring busses from Amsterdam, winking silver in the sun with their millions of tiny fish. And at night there was a sound that at first kept her awake—the croaking of giant frogs "which made a ringing noise." Nothing like them in old Gravesend!

When the town was half finished, trouble with the "aborigines" began, sporadic and unaccountable. Lady Deborah put down the fitful throwing of firebrands and such to individual mavericks and asked General Kieft for more guards, which he sent. What she could not imagine was the general's deepseated resentment of everything English, a resentment that perhaps he himself was not wholly aware of, but that made him—today one would say "subconsciously"—encourage the Indians to harass an English settlement in the middle of his Dutch territory. Later would come more conscious and deadly efforts.

Meanwhile at Gravesend there had arrived the "poor waif" who turned out to be a Dutch girl named Penelope van Princes. After being shipwrecked, widowed, scalped, and taken prisoner by Indians, it was a wonder she was alive. Apparently her youth and good health had saved her. Her hair was now a soft blonde halo around her head; and already one of Lady Deborah's young guards was interested in her!

He was Richard Stout, an Englishman who had been one of Kieft's guards for about a year, but having heard of a new community of Englishmen he was interested in joining it. Accordingly, Richard Stout was allotted a "plantation," Lot No. 18 in Gravesend, was made a guard in Lady Moody's "army," given a red uniform and a newly invented firing piece, a case of which Lady Deborah had ordered from the place of its invention, Pistola, Italy. More than his name and birthplace Lady Deborah had not inquired of Richard Stout, but she was soon to be told.

Penelope was living under her roof until more permanent arrangements could be made; soon, Stout came calling; and soon Penelope was appearing at the dinner table with shining eyes. Richard Stout hadn't just been *born* in 1610 in Nottingham, but had a ninth-century castle as the view from his bedroom window, and as a boy he had read stories about "Robyn Hode" and had hiked in Sherwood Forest. He looked fine indeed in his "fair red coat," carrying his "pis-tol" at his belt, and he said that such new "remote" weapons as these were the reason a soldier no longer needed to fight in heavy armor; was that not interesting? He had run away from home at the age of *thirty* because his father insisted on interfering with his love affairs! He joined the British Navy, where he served on a man-of-war for seven years, at the end of which time he received his discharge in New Amsterdam, so he decided to settle there; but then he heard about Lady Deborah's town and he thought he would come over here and raise tobacco and perhaps find himself a wife. . . . And he thought he would like to marry *her*. And so was she, Penelope agreed, if Lady Deborah would but give her blessing!

It must have pleased Lady Deborah to have this girl, who had been through such loss and pain, sitting in her kitchen and pouring out her heart, healed again and happy. Deborah had lost her own daughter in infancy; now here was another, grown, to take her place.

Summer, 1643, and the Indian situation began to worsen. Rumor had it that Kieft was letting his captains commit murder, loot, and rape in the Indian villages in the name of "reclaiming" stolen horses. Because of the general uneasiness, Lady Deborah felt she had better make an example of one of her guards who had gotten drunk while on duty. She wrote, "He was punished by being compelled to sit on a wooden horse during our parade, with a pitcher in one hand and a sword in the other, to show he loved beer more than his duty." She had hesitated at making the man a laughingstock, but to her relief he seemed to take it with the best of humor.

Around that same time the community had another "waif," this one a woman of middle age whose name, Anne Hutchinson, carried with it an aura of notoriety. Lady Deborah had read about her in letters from friends in Boston and Salem. Mistress Hutchinson said she was on her way to relocating herself and family in an area known as Hell Gate, just to the north of Gravesend; and did she and the other settlers have any knowledge of the way of life there?

Lady Deborah did not, but she told the Hutchinson woman about the rumors of Indian unrest.

Anne Hutchinson did not seem to "pay any mind" to this advice. She said she had never had anything but friendly associations with the Indians of Boston, and she did not expect to have any trouble with them down here!

Part II

CONFRONTATIONS

8

Hot Winds in Cold Weather

"Here it be tactful to hold one's tongue."

So had the Reverend John Cotton spoken to the new arrival in Boston in 1634, his parishioner, Anne Hutchinson, from that other Boston in England.

Anne had been a bit frightened by her reception. The two men from the ship the Hutchinson family had come over on—one of them a minister—had recommended that Anne be barred from admission to the church. They were so incensed by her claims that she was able to hear the Spirit of God through Bible verses, when everybody knew it was the minister's place to interpret God's Word, that the Reverend Cotton was obliged to seek out his senior in the church, the Reverend Wilson, and plead for Anne's acceptance. Anne did not understand what the fuss was about until Cotton explained the consequences of not being admitted. According to the terms of the Massachusetts Bay Charter, those living within its territory "shall practice no other form of divine worship than that of the Reformed (Puritan) religion"—and no one might be a member of the colony unless he belonged to that church. If Mistress Hutchinson were denied membership, she —and her family—would be banished from Boston; and there were very few other pockets of civilization where they might find shelter.

Cotton had pleaded with Mr. Wilson that this would be cruel and inhuman punishment to inflict on a family just arrived on these shores. At this, Wilson said that Mistress Hutchinson might be admitted if "at the time of her Confession she would confess to wrong thinking."

Anne wasn't surprised that she would have to make a confession; this was common practice in Puritan churches and was little more than a statement of faith in the teachings of the Church; men confessed in public, women in private. But she was surprised that Cotton said her confession must include an apology for having claimed that the Holy Spirit could speak to her directly. This, said he, was "anathama to the members of the colony." Anne felt this did not sound like her fiery Cotton from Old Boston, and in her forthright way she said so.

Cotton's answer was sobering; and did it also contain a note of fear? "Here members of the Church have suffered whippings for having a whim of their own." And now even a minister was found to have beliefs at variance with those of the Church, and the governor and magistrates meant to bring him to trial.

The name of this man was Roger Williams.

"He declares that civil magistrates have no power over matters of conscience." So wrote Governor John Winthrop in his chilly study in the diary he was to keep daily from his arrival in 1630 to his death nineteen years later. He wrote in a small cramped hand to save space, since all paper had to be ordered from England; a small hand, but the goose-quill pen had borne down so hard upon the page that often the strokes struck through.

So! This Roger Williams claimed that magistrates had no authority over a man's conscience! Well then, who did? The magistrates were elected by the ministers, and were as much a part of the Church as the ministers. Back in England (where Winthrop had lived under Elizabeth, James I, and Charles I), the Puritan government was a matter of God, king, and Church, with magistrates and ministers interpreting the Word of God—the Bible—to the common people. Here in New England the Puritan government was ruled by God, and, under Him, the Church—all else the same. This was the system of governing handed straight down from the Israelites after the Exodus from their slavery in Egypt under a worldly prince. God was their ruler now, and prophets such as Moses their preachers. This government of *theocracy* was the only one that made "divine sense"; all others were loathsome in the sight of God. And now along came this Williams, wanting to give the people freedom of conscience, instead of obeying God's ordained ministers and their civil magistrates. Governor Winthrop could see with terrible clarity where *that* would lead; directly to a separation of Church and State. No longer would there be a theocracy, but—something out of the ancient Greek or pagan ways— a *democracy!*

In such a government, any man, ignorant though he might be, would be at liberty to interpret the Bible as he saw fit. The Ten Commandments, for example. *Thou shalt not kill—* oh, this would not apply to him if his wife were dying of a loathsome disease and pleaded to be put out of her misery (as was the case with one Jonathan Twayne, having thereafter been whipped, his hands and ears cut off, and then hanged for this monstrous sin). Or a man might say "an eye for an eye" was but symbolic speech, whereas the ministers interpret it correctly to be God's implacable demand for justice. Still another puffed-up man might argue that an eye for an eye is contradicted by the Bible also saying, "If a man strike you, turn the other cheek," whereas we, the magistrates and ministers, have found explanations for all such apparent contradictions, out of our years of searching for His true interpretation; and now all this is to be challenged by this Williams, a foolish and willful democrat? He has been shipped up the coast to us from the Plimouth Colony and now we know why —his troublesome ideas could have found little favor with *their* governor!

Governor Winthrop of the Massachusetts Bay Colony, sitting in his bleak study that winter of 1634, made a last entry for the day. Still another potential troublemaker had been set down in their midst—and she a mere woman. "A Mistress Hutchinson." Before she was even off the ship, "she had begun to set forth her own stuff." Mr. Cotton, her minister, had affirmed that she would "cease and desist."

Anne's confession was conducted by Cotton's superior, the Reverend John Wilson, a man she was later to call crude and to whom she had taken an instant dislike. Because of this, when Wilson asked her to repudiate her statement that God's Spirit spoke directly to her through the Bible, she took pleasure in outwitting him. Referring—in her own conscience —to domestic errors of judgment over years of marriage, she replied, "I have been guilty of wrong thinking," and felt a sting of triumph when this was accepted and she was admitted to the Church.

Easy triumphs can lull one into a false sense of security. And Anne felt indeed secure and content that first winter in Boston. She was again near her beloved Reverend Cotton. Her husband, Will, had started up a profitable new business in woolens. Her children were all in good health. And she and Will had moved into a large house, near that of Captain John Underhill of the Massachusetts Militia, and across from the only house made of brick in Boston, belonging to William Coddington, the colony's treasurer. Both men, and Governor Winthrop as well, had paid calls on Mistress Hutchinson. Anne found Coddington a balding, worried-looking man who nonetheless seemed genuinely glad to see such a "fine brood of new-blood to nourish our small band"; Captain Underhill had a fierce manner and a moustache to match, but he brought painted wooden soldiers and sweetmeats of maple sugar for her younger children. As for the governor, a nervous man who gave her a rather piercing stare, he declined to sit down and stayed only a few minutes, saying little except that he wished her "a peaceable and trouble-free existence here."

And why should she not enjoy just that? Before the end of the long winter she had become known to everyone and appreciated much for "her kindly ministrations in time of illness, her skill in nursing, her cheerful neighboring and willingness to assist in birthings," wrote a chronicler of the time. She also ministered to Indian women who came to her house with sick babies. Anne Hutchinson had time, patience, and love enough for everyone.

A long winter, 1634–1635, and, in the opinion of settlers who had endured four others since the colony's beginnings, the hardest yet. Nobody could remember such gripping winters back in the old country. "From Nov. 2 to March 29, snow flakes the size of shillings," wrote the governor in his diary. Frostbite blackened many a finger and toe on even short excursions into the forests for firewood. And in all those long months—aside from domestic chores and the vigilance needed to protect themselves from prowling wolves, fires, and Indians—the Boston Puritans permitted themselves practically nothing else to do. They worked, went to church, came home and read—in their Bible. On Sundays they could not even work. The governor had found plenty of examples of God's wrath at men who dared lift a finger on the Sabbath:

Archibald Thomson of Marble Head, carrying dung to his Garden in a Canoe on the Lord's Day in fair Weather and Still Water it sank under him in the Harbor near Shore and he was never seen after.

Nothing to do. A man could not even go out and get drunk; and in his own house, if he took more than one or two drinks, he was in danger of his wife's mentioning it, and it would get to his minister. The ministers had also come out against "that sophisticated trait, the drinking of toasts, as it flatters other men, not God." A long winter's evening would have been eased by the smoking of tobacco; it too was frowned on; and that recent device of the Devil, the taking of snuff, was "to cloud the mind as a drug, an unnatural act in God's sight." This little group of people, having voluntarily cut themselves off from almost every available source of culture and civilization, now further denied themselves the most innocent of pleasures such as might have been derived from the organizing of a choir for hymn singing, or putting on morality plays, or having contests—baking or sewing among the women, feats of strength among the men, and among the children, drawing or spelling bees. *Pleasure*, that was the word that stopped them from even considering such activities. A few months ago, in the autumn, after the crops of corn and rye had been especially good, and fish and game found in plenty, some of the younger members had wanted to observe a "Thanks-giving." The magistrates would have given permission had these people had in mind a purely religious observance of the giving of thanks to God, as had that brave band on the first Thanks-giving in Jamestown in 1610 after the "Starving Winter." But no, these young Puritans wanted to emulate the "pyoneers of the Plimouth Plantation," who, in autumn 1621, had lost their perspective and joined in with the annual Indian harvest festivities with roasted goose, venison, turkey, eels, salmon, and the fermented juice of apples. Surely this sight was displeasing in the eyes of the Lord.

Even the holy days were no cause for celebration. (And here all Puritans agreed.) The most important season, Easter, which began with Lent (the Old English word for spring) seven weeks before, was observed by fasting. On Easter they dressed in their dark-brown best and sat through longer than the customary two-hour sermons, morning and evening. Seven weeks later came the end of the season, known as Pentecost— originally a Hebraic harvest feast signifying the "penta," or fiftieth, week of the year, but misinterpreted by Christian translators as "penitent." The Puritans did penance by sitting up all night on bare benches in unheated churches in silent prayer.

They did not observe the December birthday of Jesus, "Christ's Mass"; for the word Mass carried with it a Catholic stigma, and, besides, the custom had its roots in ancient celebrations, pagan sacrifices to sun or fertility gods, with rites around a wassail bowl and the burning of Yule logs in the worship of trees. The Puritans did not worship trees; all Nature, in fact, was opposed to God, a physical snare and distraction, the admiration of which denied a jealous God the total attention He demanded. All men were born in Adam's Original Sin; the world itself was under a divine curse, life on earth but a time of test to see whether, on Judgment Day, a man would go to heaven or hell.

Nothing—to—do! A man could not even relieve pent-up emotions with a string of expletives, at least not within earshot of anybody else. The governor had found awesome examples of God's immediate vengeance:

. . . the *Mary Rolfe* from Bristol, 200 tons, blew up in Boston Harbor with her own powder, about 200 barrels, because the Capt and crew had been profaning the name of God and laughed at some protestors of this, on the wharf. The protestors escaped. Praise be to God.

Nothing. To. Do. And finally the men of the colony found *something* to do. They started holding meetings on weekday afternoons for the purpose of discussing the sermons of the previous Sunday. Women, of course, were excluded.

These meetings went along well enough until about the fourth or fifth one, when the subject matter widened to include discussion of the "Puritan Revolution" now raging in England, Protestants against Charles I. Then arguments and fist fights erupted.

Meanwhile, the shut-out women of the colony were beginning to hold meetings themselves at the house of Mistress Hutchinson—not to get even with the men, but because Anne Hutchinson was stimulating to talk with and had such interesting ideas. Their own husbands would never discuss religious matters with them—which amounted to discussing nothing at all—whereas Anne answered their questions and treated even the women younger than herself with respect for their intelligence.

It was Anne's idea, then, to do something more with these meetings than just talk; each woman should bring along whatever she was working on, such as a rag rug or a quilt. The suggestion was met with delight, and by the time the long winter softened into spring, some sixty women were coming regularly to Anne's hospitable house, their hands busy turning old dark-green, navy-blue and brown garments into beautifully patterned quilts, and their minds engaged in working out some fascinating point in the Bible.

Anne Hutchinson had found something to do. She had also, inadvertently, founded the first women's club in America. And perhaps she deserves credit for inventing the quilting bee.

The men's meetings had broken up, leaving sour feelings and bitter feuds. Hearing of the meetings to which their wives were going, at first they had dismissed them as "woman stuff, a gaggle of gossips." But then the wives began coming home with religious ideas of their own—some of which were lodged in the heads of their husbands who had not dared consider voicing them! This Hutchinson female—what was she teaching those others, most of them younger than she and more likely to be swayed by her opinions? Get her minister to go see her and put an end to this nonsense.

Anne was delighted at this unexpected visit by her Reverend Cotton. He said he had come to ask her about the weekly meetings she was holding with many of the women in the colony. Just what did they all find to talk about?

She answered willingly. It was mainly the sermons of the preceding Sunday, the way the men did when they got together. Especially Mr. Cotton's own sermons. "Most of the women are in agreement, that of all the ministers we have heard, none preaches the Covenant of Grace so sweetly as does Mr. Cotton!"

Cotton thanked her for her "opinion," but assured her that all the ministers preached with an equal access to God's grace.

Oh, no, Anne answered him readily. His superior, Mr. Wilson, preached nothing but form and ceremony, "naught but the Covenant of Works."

Cotton was shocked. To say a minister preached only the Covenant of Works was the same as saying he had no spirit of God within him, therefore he could not interpret God's Word to his congregation. He said, "That is as serious a charge as if to say, 'My teacher is struck dumb.'" What else did Mistress Hutchinson and her women discuss?

Why, said Anne, that each of them had the Holy Spirit within herself, and when hard-pressed, they had but to open their Bibles and God might speak to them directly through His Word.

Cotton could hardly believe his ears. He said she must not preach such things any more. It was the purpose of the ministers to interpret the Word. "There has been much muttering that you are affecting the hearts of the younger women with dangerous new principles."

It was Anne's turn to be surprised. These ladies were so grateful for her help. Most of them had not realized the Holy Spirit could communicate with them. What a comfort, when they were most of them so lonely, having left a portion of themselves—homes, parents, friends—so far behind, never to behold again in this world!

Cotton said in a kind but stern manner that Mistress Hutchinson must cease and desist from all such talk, forthwith. Anne's mood brightened.

"Oh, we are talking of something else now, Mr. Cotton. The recent trial and banishment of Roger Williams!"

The controversial figure of this great Puritan, with his audacious talk of the separation of Church and State, had promised a fresh wind of change, of personal freedom. But after a trial that the men of the colony said was "a grand spectacle" and "an all-day sparring match," Williams had been banished with his supporters; and many were the ones who felt the colony the poorer for it. This included most of the women, who were also dismayed at the wave of violence the banishment had brought on.

Upon the broad and grassy reaches of Boston Common, originally set aside "for the trayning Field and the feeding of Cattel," a proclamation had been posted: The first offense against religious difference of opinion should be a severe public reprimand; the second, a fine of five pounds (half a year's wages); the third, to stand on a high block with a sign on the chest, "I Have Synned." Men guilty of pro-Williams sympathies had been chained to two dwarfed and twisted elms that hunched among other tall straight trees—as symbol of their own "mis-direction." Two women, Mary Tompkins and Alice Ambrose, had voiced disapproval of their minister's way of teaching and had been driven by horse and wagon through thirteen towns in the territory, receiving ten whiplashes in each; a member of Anne's own group had been rumored to "give lieing sexual remarks about her minister," and had suffered "a stick stuck through her tongue." There was a swelling of attendance at the Hutchinson house.

Soon John Cotton paid Anne a second visit, this time with a bound volume he presented to her, excerpts of his own sermons which had been translated by another minister who worked closely with the Indians, and "written in the phonetic of the Algonkin Massachusetts Tribe for the purpose of teaching Christianity to these poor savages for the saving of their souls."

Milk for Babes, Drawn Out of the Breasts of Both Testaments Chiefly for the Spiritual Nourishment of Boston Babes in Either England for Their Souls' Nourishment. But may be read by any Christian Child.

by John Cotton, Divine

The first lines read: "Massachuset Up—Biblum God Nukkone—Testament Nashauanittus Jesus Meninnunk . . ."

"Now, Mistress Hutchinson," continued Cotton, "with this book, this primer for teaching the Indians about Christ, *you* can read to those salvages you have nursed and befriended, and bring them unto the Lord. Can you think of a more worthy calling for a Puritan who is not an ordained minister, and not even a man?"

Anne thanked him for the book and promised to communicate with her dark-skinned friends. But now, if he would excuse her, some women had just come in and were full of news over the latest atrocities on Boston Common. . . !

9

"An American Jezebel"

Excerpts from Governor Winthrop's diary in 1630 and 1631:

> The Governor's wife and family arrived from England this day after ten weeks at sea, and lost none of their company but two children, whereof one was the Governor's daughter Anne, age about 1½ years. . . . The Governor's son Henry drowned this day at Salem.

Always referring to himself in the third person, Governor Winthrop permitted himself only a statement of fact when it came to events in his personal life. He also did not spare himself if he made errors in judgment that were apparent to him, as evinced by one of the entries in his neat and detailed Index: "How the Governor went out in the Woods at Dusk and was lost all Night until Sunrise." It was only in matters pertaining to his responsibilities as leader of the colony that Winthrop allowed a bit of emotion to creep into the record. Nobody appreciated the troubles of a colonial governor in the wilderness—except God. Yes, God was forever sending him, John Winthrop, direct signs of His close surveillance of the Massachusetts Bay Colony. Even to the machinations of mice.

Another Mr. Winthrop, a Magistrate, had a copy of the New Testament, and book of common prayer and the Psalms bound together. And these three books kept in' an Outhouse where Corn was stored. The book of common prayer was eaten, every page, by Mice, but neither Holy Books were touched. Praise be to God.

There was comfort in such intimate attention, but fear also. For if ill fate befell the sheep in this fold, who would be blamed before God? Their shepherd. Those aforementioned mice could also be regarded as malevolent, either sent by the Devil, or possibly by God as a test—since they just could not be kept out of the winter grain stores. In their rodent way they were as great a threat as the wolves who kept breaking into the meat holds. Shall we all survive another long and bitter winter without famine taking off our old and infirm? As for our most stalwart, the salvages are taking care of them. Some Indian villages were friendly, but they could turncoat in a day, over a fancied grievance. And when they did turn on the settlers they did not fight fairly, as white men did, in proper uniform, advancing in orderly ranks with brave and forthright purpose; they skulked in the forests or took to the hills and from behind a boulder would pick off a man here, a woman or child there, no matter! Last week they had put a snake-venom arrow through the shoulder of a guard as he walked the parapet of our poor unfinished fort—dead before his body struck the ground. And it will grow worse, for now up and down the coast they are being sold firearms by the Dutch. Damn the salvages and damn Willem Kieft, sitting down there in New Amsterdam in his fine finished fort and ringed 'round by his city wall!

Next the governor permitted himself a few uncharitable

thoughts about the "Plimouth Plantation." A proof of the character of that Separatist rabble lay in the fact that their Captain Myles Standish had already been obliged to arrest two men for murder, one of them his own deputy, John Alden; next he had arrested and sent to England to stand trial a certain colonist named Thomas Morton, for having "harbored runaway Slaves, sold Guns to the Indians . . . and erected a May Pole around which he danced to celebrate the coming of Spring." In England, Sir Ferdinando Gorges had discovered this Morton had legal training, so instead of clapping him into jail he had retained him as a counsel to try to "void the Massachusetts Bay Charter"!

Ever since the very year of its birth, Sir Ferdinando had been trying to have the charter declared "irregular." His excuse, he had written the governor, was that it was not exact as to its land grants, which were "from three miles north of the Merrimac River to three miles south of the Charles River," and within those north-south boundaries, "from Sea to Sea." Now, what could be more precise than that? The governor had settled Boston legally therein—and everybody knew how far it was from the Atlantic to the Pacific Ocean. Balboa, discovering the Pacific in 1514, and Verrazano, exploring the Atlantic coast in 1521, had both agreed on this.

The Atlantic and the Pacific were forty miles apart.

Governor Winthrop knew this and so, he knew, did Sir Ferdinando Gorges. And Winthrop also knew the real reason that the "Proprietor of Main" was trying to break the charter. He wanted to make all of New-England a royal colony. Well, Winthrop would fight that tooth and nail, to keep his colony under God—and John Winthrop!

And today there had sailed into Boston harbor the man he would have to fight. Morton apparently not having had much luck at so far a remove, Gorges had now sent a representative of high position to conduct an inquisition on the spot. His name was Sir Henry Vane.

Historians would say later of this man that he was one of the greatest Puritan statesmen of the age, spiritually akin to Jefferson and Samuel Adams. It is doubtful whether Governor Winthrop could afford to be half so generous. Not only did Vane represent Sir Ferdinando and peril to the charter, but in person he was a living and breathing affront. He had strode off the ship that morning, a plume in his tricorne—gallantly swept off for the ladies—and sporting a well-trimmed beard and spurs on his polished boots—after two months at sea! A product of Oxford, he had represented England at her embassy in Vienna. He was fluent in French and German. He had not yet celebrated his twenty-third birthday.

John Winthrop, Cambridge, attorney, aged forty-seven, could not help noticing with what admiration Sir Henry Vane was greeted in *his* colony. And now, after midnight, he could not sleep and so turned to his diary. Also off the *Griffin* this voyage had come a Reverend Wheelwright, silenced minister and brother-in-law of Mistress Anne Hutchinson; also, one Mary Dyer, friend of Mistress H.'s, who had the temerity to disembark wearing a gray gown, the garb of a Quaker! Mistress H. "continues to hold her seditious meetings." The governor would send a delegation of the ministers to her. They should remind her of the banishment of Roger Williams, and that "she is in Danger of Trial herself."

"Also the *Griffin* did neglect to fill order of Limes. Shall we all perish of Scurvey this Winter, who shall be blamed? . . ."

Anne Hutchinson's big house was noisy with laughter and cheer. How good it was to see the homely face of John Wheelwright again, and the pert smile of her dear friend Mary Dyer. What a lot of news there was to catch up with. For her part, Anne showed off Zuriel, her two-month-old boy.

Anne assured her brother-in-law that there would be a church for him in one of the towns around Massachusetts

Bay. And to Mary, that she would become a member of her own, Anne's, congregation, to enjoy the sermons of Mr. Cotton. But that she had "better put off the gray. They are not tolerant of the Quaker habit here." Mary assured Anne she was only a Quaker sympathizer, for their quiet, simple ways. Anne laughed. Mary would soon learn, everything here was either *for* or *against;* no shadings of opinion allowed!

Yet the next day, when a delegation of ministers arrived and politely asked if they might question her about her beliefs, Anne Hutchinson never thought to apply that *for* or *against* to herself.

Why, yes, she was still holding the women's meetings. Young women such as her friend Mistress Dyer, just come from England, were much comforted to know that the Holy Spirit dwelt within them, instead of having always to hear Him through the mouth of some minister who, excellent though he might be, would be unknown to them, strangers in these parts! At that moment Mary Dyer happened to put in an appearance, still dressed in that unacceptable gray. . . .

The ministers (Cotton remaining silent) proceeded with patience. If she believed the Spirit spoke directly to a person, she was denying the principal tenet of the Reformed Religion—that only through the Bible could God's Word be heard, and only through the interpretation of ordained ministers could ordinary folk understand that meaning. Anne looked placid—and unconvinced.

It was so simple and clear to them. With the greatest of earnestness they proceeded to make sure she understood the steps that had led them to where they were, in the enlightened year 1636.

In 1374 John Wycliffe, the first Puritan, had fought the Pope to establish his beliefs that Scripture, and not the priests, revealed the Word of God. He paved the way for Martin Luther and the Reformation, at which time the Bible was revised from its old errors corrupted by the Church of Rome.

John Calvin made later refinements of meaning; since then, two generations of Puritans had refined Calvin's interpretations, until this, the King James Version, was "now, finally and forevermore, the Truth." And so it was not right for Mistress Hutchinson to believe or teach others that *she* had the Truth, when obviously it was to be found only in the King James Version, as interpreted by her ministers. In so doing, she was throwing out all that the Puritans believed in and had fought so hard for, for the last three hundred years!

Well, said Anne, it did seem to her that if Luther had revised the Bible, and Calvin after him, and then two generations of Puritans, and now King James, that it was just possibly *not* the final interpretation. And in fact, she had heard varying interpretations of the same point of Scripture from ministers in this very room. So why was she not just as qualified to listen to the Voice within herself?

Gasps of dismay. Then Mr. Wilson, Cotton's superior, asked: If Mistress Hutchinson believed the Spirit spoke to her directly, of what use were the ministers?

Anne's answer was quick and bright as she turned toward Cotton. Oh, she would never want to be without the inspiration of *some* ministers. Why, she had come all the way from England so as not to be deprived of the spiritual grace of Mr. Cotton's sermons!

It was Mr. Wilson who pressed on to the final question. If Mistress Hutchinson did not believe in the need for most ministers, that is, the Church, then would she not also do away with the State? For what was the State without religion? All were one, under God!

It was perhaps the first time that Anne had been brought face to face with the logical end results of her claiming that God gave her a sign when she needed one. And for once in her life she kept silent. Perhaps, finally, she felt a spark of fright.

The ministers began leaving. John Cotton took Anne briefly

aside. The ministers had been sent to her by Governor Winthrop. Now, this was serious. She must give up absolutely her meetings. Did she understand? Anne did.

And she must "give *no public statement* of her beliefs." Did she understand? Anne did.

Cotton looked a bit relieved. Perhaps, after all, the matter would blow over. The governor was facing a new election. By the time it was over, he might forget about Mistress Hutchinson's need for the counsel of every minister in Boston.

For all his complaining over the terrible responsibilities of being the first governor of Massachusetts, there is no doubt that John Winthrop expected to become also its second one.

Election Day, and the magistrates and ministers assembled in the General Court at New Town (later, Cambridge) outside Boston, to vote on their officers and governor for the next two years. Winthrop waited it out at home. And thought of Sir Henry Vane, probably at his own house, poring over the Massachusetts Bay Charter with his clever diplomat's eyes, so experienced in Continental wiles. Some trick learned at the Vienna court to shatter the fragile bulwark of his, Winthrop's, fledgling colony? A monstrous thought . . .

From Winthrop's study, a commotion below. The magistrates, come to give him the news. He went down.

His officials were looking not so much pleased as relieved. They had voted *en masse*, and persuaded the less politically minded ministers to follow suit. Well, they hoped the, ah, governor would understand their reasoning. The best way to keep Sir Henry Vane from digging into the legality of the charter was to make *him* head of its domain.

It made such beautiful sense, it was enough to make an ex-governor ill.

On January 29, 1637, a fast day, the newly ordained Reverend Wheelwright gave his first sermon at the church at

Mt. Wollaston (later, Quincy). It was attended by Deputy Governor Winthrop and all eighteen of his magistrates, none of whom, of course, had eaten breakfast nor would they partake of any nourishment until sunup of the next morning. Wheelwright, to their astonishment, preached against fasting, saying, "We should only fast in penitence when we feel the spirit of Christ is not present within this Church." To go without food for twenty-four hours, and get no credit for it! Next day the minister was summoned to the governor's chambers. A reprimand. The delegation had detected "more than a hint of Mistress Hutchinson's heresies in the sermon."

Wheelwright's sermon tone did not change. On March 9, without a day's notice, he was summoned to the General Court and tried for contempt, and forbidden to preach while sentence was suspended.

Anne was very upset; her women friends urged her to start a petition for the exoneration of Wheelwright's reputation. Anne drafted the paper and some sixty women signed it. Then Cotton appeared, cautioning Anne not to add her own signature. She was "already under a dark enough cloud." Next came the announcement that "the weapons of all friends of said Wheelwright shall be seized."

Weapons! Anne Hutchinson did not believe in bearing arms and had so persuaded her husband. There wasn't a musket or sword in the Hutchinson-Wheelwright family; and Wheelwright had no other "friends" as yet in Boston. Now, this no-arms pacifism led to further trouble. A war was building with the Pequot Indians, and the magistrates were dismayed to find that several colonists refused to ride off with Captain Underhill and shoot Indians because Mistress Hutchinson had convinced first their wives, then themselves, that God did not approve of Puritans killing other men.

Anne and Will Hutchinson stayed in their house most evenings now, sensing a town gradually turning against them.

Early in October, little Zuriel was seized with spasms, and died.

Wheelwright's petition had been signed by young William Dyer, husband of Mary. He was summoned to court, and "fined and disgraced."

Mary Dyer was five months pregnant, and had been sickly during most of this period. The death of Anne's child had affected her, and now this public disgrace of her husband! A few days later she went into an early labor. Anne, herself a midwife, did not trust her amateur's abilities in a case of premature birth. She sent in haste for the Widow Hawkins. This was a toothless crone who had a reputation of offering oil of mandrake root to encourage pregnancy, the root being shaped like the legs and trunk of a human; a queer but competent soul; she had delivered Anne of her Zuriel.

Widow Hawkins was closeted with Mary for a long time, during which Anne tried to keep her mind off poor Mary's screams; then she heard a deep groan, and all was still.

The midwife emerged. She had delivered a still-birth that was a "monster"—a hideously misshapen little body. In terror the widow begged Anne to help her bury it before anyone else found it. A monster birth was God's most awful sign of disapproval of anybody connected with it!

Not knowing what else to do—certainly not wanting Mary to see the creature—Anne went with the widow into nearby woods; there, hoping not to be seen, they buried the body.

But they were seen—by a man whose wife had been attending meetings at the Hutchinson house in spite of his stern forbidding. He waited until the women had gone, then came and dug up the body. When he saw what he uncovered, he put it back again in horror, and went and told some of his friends. These men remembered that just recently Mistress Hutchinson's own child had "been taken." They put one and one together and came up with the presence of—a Devil in the town, who had got both Mistress Hutchinson and her friend Mary

Dyer pregnant in order to corrupt the town in God's eyes. Now they must go tell the governor what they had found. They started for the house of Sir Henry Vane but something stopped them. Winthrop was still governor in their minds. As for Sir Henry Vane . . . with that pointed beard, plumed hat, and spurs, hadn't people *said* he had a devil-may-care look about him?

Winthrop ordered the body exhumed, then sent for the Widow Hawkins, whom he questioned so long and closely that she was sure she was bound for the stake. Yes, sir, it wanted to come out wrong. Sideways, it seemed. She begged to be forgiven, she would never attend any other women again.

"Midwife Hawkins is banished from the colony, but will bear watching," Winthrop wrote, "as it is suspected she is a witch. . . . The creature came hiplings until she turned it. It had a face but no head, and the ears stood upon the shoulders. . . ."

Next order of business: the rumor that Sir Henry Vane was the Devil, or his agent, and had fathered the monster and Mistress Hutchinson's dead child. Certainly Vane's arrival had seemed to carry a whiff of the diabolic as far as John Winthrop was concerned. But the ex-governor was not so easily persuaded. Two months earlier, a certain John Herverd, or Harverd, had died, leaving half of his estate, the sum of 779 pounds, for the founding of ". . . a new Colledge for the Perpetration of the Glory and Teachings of Christ Jesus," and committed to the Ptolemaic theory that the Earth was the center of the universe. Sir Henry Vane had helped speed the release and application of this kind behest, and in Christ's name had proposed the college be named after this patron— Hervard. Therefore it was clear that Vane was not a devil's agent; but Winthrop was not fooled. A devil *was* afoot in Boston. And his signs could no longer be ignored.

Winthrop reminded himself again of his responsibilities as a sort of latter-day Moses. "For the Lord has chosen these people the Puritans and led them across the great Sea to the Promised Land of 'Israel,' and because we are the Chosen we can not sin at so cheap a rate [as others]. If we perform, God will preserve our estate; if not, he will abandon and ex-terminate us."

And then the ex-governor let out his full feelings about Mistress Hutchinson. A woman not content to stay a house-keeper! "She hath lost her wits by giving herself to reading and writing." A woman who dared forbid her menfolk to bear arms! "She, contrary to Scripture, rules the Roost." A woman whose words were proud and haughty! "She hath so orgulus a Mind." A woman whose willful ways had made her "go a-whoring from God. She is an American Jezebel.

"She shall be tried as an Heretic."

10

The Trial

UNEXPECTED ALLIES

Shortly after sunup on a morning in late October the paper was slapped with glue upon the Hutchinson door, to be discovered by Will, patient and perhaps long-suffering Will Hutchinson, whose duty he felt it was to pry it off as best he could and take it up to his wife.

Anne had been staying in bed late in the last few weeks, often until six thirty. She was again pregnant, and still grieving over the death of Zuriel and the tragedy of Mary Dyer's miscarriage. In stalked Will, holding the paper as if it were burning his hand. Anne read her own name in large, ominous black letters:

Mrs. Anne Hutchinson, of Boston, Massachusetts Bay Colony,
For Moving against Public Law and Order and the
Tranquillity of the State

PROCLAMATION OF SESSIONS
at General Court, New Town, 2 November 1637.

HENRY VANE, BART., Govr.
JOHN WINTHROP, DEP. Govr.

This was terrible, said Will. He would write a petition against it and take it around Boston. All over the territory! A hundred signatures and Henry Vane would not dare to move against a good and blameless woman.

Anne thanked her husband, and he went lunging downstairs to search for writing materials. Anne lay back on her pillow. Sir Henry Vane? Oh, no. John Winthrop was her enemy, because of the meetings. As for the petition, Anne knew how much good a petition had done for Brother Wheelwright.

Winthrop meant to have her banished. He had done it to Roger Williams.

To banish her, and her family. She fought down panic; it was really too much to think about. One of the girls—Susannah?—was crying in the next room. Time to be up and about, and keep busy!

Will Hutchinson took his petition all over, to Boston and Mt. Wollaston and Roxbury and the other towns of the territory, trudging from house to house—a horse being no good for this job—assuring folk that his wife was "a dear saint and a servant of God." But most people would not sign; they said they knew and loved Anne Hutchinson but were afraid to put down their names because of reprisals such as had been made against William Dyer.

Anne assured her husband that a petition with hundreds of names on it would probably do no good. The trial would be open-and-shut. And Will knew as well as she that there would be no representative for the accused, who would be assumed to be guilty unless she could prove her innocence. Anne would be confronted with hostile witnesses but have no right to witnesses in her favor. There would be no jury of her peers, only the decision of the judges after hearing both "sides"—that of the accused and that of the body of accusers.

Two days before the trial Anne had unexpected visitors: Sir Henry Vane, Captain John Underhill, and William Coddington. These gentlemen declared they had made their positions plain to the deputy governor, the magistrates, and most of the ministers. Said Sir Henry, the Massachusetts Bay Charter had not been cleared for its validity, yet he had not been able in so short a time to disprove it, and so—! He had been obliged to affix his name to the proclamation and would preside as judge, but would try to lend support to Mistress Hutchinson, with whom he had no quarrel, by his nonparticipation. And, unlike the trial of Roger Williams, "this shall be no cut-and-dried affair. Your accusers shall be obliged to prove their points."

Next, Captain Underhill, recently returned from his skirmishes with the Pequots, spoke up. He said he had not much use for ministers, being a rough fighting man for God, and he did not like to see women, especially mothers, publicly threatened and humiliated. He had just put to the sword several whole Indian villages, and before he came to the New World he had fought for the king in Catholic Spain; but when it came to Puritan womanhood he would defend their honor with his life.

Then it was the turn of Treasurer Coddington. He said only that he was in agreement with the governor.

Anne thanked the three men warmly and they left. A few moments later William Coddington was back. Alone with Anne he confessed he was "a secret Quaker" since coming to Boston and realizing the "narrowing influence of ministers on the Word of God." He would not dare confess this even to loyal friends, but Mistress Dyer had approached him and begged him at least not to give testimony against Mistress

Hutchinson. So, in spite of feared reprisals, he would show his sympathies by remaining silent, for he hoped "this trial will help break through the crust of formalism hardening over religion, and allow the springs of natural piety to well to the surface and refresh the arid theology of these times."

Anne was immensely heartened, and went to see Mary Dyer to thank her for speaking to Coddington. She found her young friend much changed—pale and hollow eyed, with a shrill, nervous manner. Anne hoped she would soon recover and become her pretty, vivacious self.

Mary was excited to hear of the promise of three men of power, that they were in Anne's corner. So she made up a list of "for" and "against." In the 'for" column she wrote the names of Vane, Coddington, and Underhill. In the "against" went Deputy Governor Winthrop, all eighteen of his magistrates, and eight of the nine ministers—Wheelwright would not be allowed in court. And straddling the line—the name of John Cotton.

At Anne's shocked expression, she said, "You cannot count on Cotton. He is a trimmer. He is as lief to deny you as not, if he feels his own position threatened."

Then Mary encouraged Anne to prepare her defense. The charges were vague in the extreme, to make this well-nigh impossible, but Mary was sure Anne would have to answer for those famous meetings in which she played the role of teacher. So, well into the night, she and Anne would consult their Bibles. That was what the other side would be doing!

ACCUSATION, REBUTTAL

November 2, 1637, noon. The bell in the New Town Court clanged. The double doors were thrown open and a crowd of some two hundred persons surged in, jostling and shouting. Everyone wanted to sit in the first rows to be as near as possible to the "bench," the long table at which the judge and other officials, gowned and wigged, were already sitting, and in front of which the defendant would stand; also, they would be less cold. The only heat would be the foot warmers provided by the court's doorman (janitor)—pierced wooden boxlike containers with hot coals inside, and which were already in place beneath the table. There would be no foot warmer for the defendant.

Here she came now, down the center aisle, Mistress Hutchinson, guided by her minister, John Cotton.

Anne was all in black in mourning for her dead child, but she held her head high and did not lean unduly on Cotton's arm. Directly behind these two came Mary Dyer, with her hand just touching Anne's shoulder—a daring association no one else in the room would risk. Yet perhaps the support of Mary Dyer was not an unmixed blessing. For upon setting eyes on her, people were whispering, "That is the woman that had the monster."

Seated at one end of the bench as judge, Sir Henry Vane motioned to the bailiff to pound for order with his kevel (later, gavel—a ship's wooden belaying peg).

A large gold-edged Bible lay open in the center of the table; the bailiff asked Anne to lay her right hand upon it and swear that the testimony she would give was "Truth, whole Truth, naught but Truth. So help you, God." Anne swore.

As she did, she noticed the book was open to St. Matthew, Chapter V—the Sermon on the Mount. In an instant her practiced glance had flown down to Verse 10; "Blessed are they which are persecuted for righteousness: for theirs is the kingdom of Heaven."

She was sure it was a sign; and why not, in this, her hour of direst need, when so many times before the Holy Spirit had found His Way to speak to her!

The part of Sir Henry Vane in the trial was to open the proceedings and to close them, finally, with the verdict. Now he gave a calm, sanguine look over a little clump of papers before him and spoke without emphasis. Mistress Hutchinson was accused of eighty-two "errors in conduct and belief." Four were major and were as follows: One: She was accused of "consorting with those that had been sowers of sedition." Two: She had broken the Fifth Commandment. Three: She was accused of claiming revelation of God's Word directly. Four: She had misrepresented the conduct of the ministers.

Anne stood before this long table of men in a temporary daze. Even with the empathy she sensed in Sir Henry's voice, she did not know what most of those accusations meant!

Now it was the turn of the accused's own minister to put in a plea on her behalf. It must have been a comfort for Anne at that moment to hear John Cotton's voice:

"We beseech you to remember the old method of Satan, who has raised up such calumnies against the faithful prophets of God, in His very Words. Elijah was called the trouble of Israel, 1 Kings 18:17,18. Amos was charged for conspiracy, Amos 7:10. Paul was counted a pestilent fellow, a mover of sedition and a ring leader of a sect, Acts 24:5. Christ Himself . . . was charged to be a teacher of a new doctrine. Now we beseech you, consider whether that old serpent work not after his old method even in our days." He seemed about to sit down—perhaps there was something in Anne Hutchinson's expression that moved him to go on a little more.

"Let all things be done in love; proceed with patience and cast not off as reprobate, such as cannot presently join with us in every point of discipline. As St. Paul enjoins us in Colossians 3:12: 'Put on therefore, as the elect of God, bowels of mercies and kindness.' " He sat down.

The questioning was led, as Anne had feared—and yet almost looked forward to!—by Deputy Governor Winthrop. From his place at the center of the table he clasped hands before him and began.

She was accused of consorting with persons condemned for sedition and therefore in a state of Coventry—that is, not to be communicated with.

ANNE: Please sir, who might these persons be?

WINTHROP: The silenced Brother Wheelwright, and others since cited for contempt of court, fined, disgraced, or banished.

Now Anne realized why her brother-in-law had been so quickly brought to trial. Her reply: "I did not sign the petition in his favor." This was not good enough. Finally, she said that it seemed difficult not to say good morning or good evening to one's own brother-in-law; and that it seemed to her that for the last several months, during which time he had been detained in custody, that he, Deputy Governor, had done more communicating with John Wheelwright than herself.

Her reply was met with gasps and yawps throughout the room. This was the sort of spirit—foregone loser putting up a fight before certain defeat—that the people had been hoping for. Something to chew over for the rest of the winter! Winthrop was holding a consultation with the magistrates. The first point had been dropped.

Next. Mistress Hutchinson had broken the Fifth Commandment. Honour thy father and thy mother.

WINTHROP: We, the ministers and magistrates, are your fathers. We forbade you to hold meetings in which you instructed women. You obeyed not our commandment.

ANNE (in effect): Agreed, Sir, that you and all of you are somehow my one father, albeit the natural one, a good minister, is dead. (She now found ready answers in two quotations that Mary Dyer had found.) I put it to you, Sir, in Acts 18:26, wherein Aquila and *his wife* Priscilla took upon themselves to instruct Apollos the Jew, a man of good parts, in the meaning of the risen Christ.

WINTHROP (quickly): See how your argument stands. Priscilla, *with her husband*, took Apollos home to instruct him privately. Therefore Mistress Hutchinson without her husband may teach sixty or seventy!

ANNE: Further, Sir. Titus 2:3–5. That the aged woman may teach the younger women. These instances in which Holy Writ permits, nay, encourages, a woman to teach are but two out of several.

WINTHROP (indicating the open Bible before Anne): A pity then, Mistress, with so many instances to choose from, you chose Titus 2. Kindly read along from your own illustration.

ANNE: ". . . that they may teach the young women to be sober, to love their husbands, to love their children, to be discreet, chaste, keepers at home, good, obedient to their own husbands, that the word of God be not blasphemed."

WINTHROP: This is not what you have taught the women that came to you.

ANNE: I called them not, but when they came I instructed them.

WINTHROP: Yet you show us not a rule.

ANNE: I have given you two places in Scripture.

WINTHROP: But neither of them will suit your practice.

ANNE: Must I show my name written therein?

At this Winthrop probably lost his temper.

WINTHROP: "But I suffer not a woman to teach,"—I Timothy 2:12—"nor to usurp authority over the man, but to be in silence. For Adam was first formed, then Eve. And Adam was not deceived, but the woman being deceived was in the wrongdoing. Notwithstanding she shall be saved in childbearing if she continue with faith and charity and holiness."

ANNE: Sir, whose voice is this speaking?

WINTHROP: Yours is not to ask the questions.

ANNE: I put it to you, this is St. Paul to the people. Just as it is Paul to the people in the Book of Acts and of Titus. In divers places Paul reports on the teachings of Priscilla, and the teaching of younger women by older, yet he suffers not a woman to teach . . .

WINTHROP: It is for the purpose of interpretation that ministers are appointed after study. Only to the ignorant and stiff-necked does God's Word appear to yield contradictions. You have set yourself up as a teacher in these matters.

ANNE: Put it, I have not been that since about September last, about the time I was ordered to desist.

Again, a murmured discussion while Anne stood waiting. Surely she had won the second point!

At any event, here came the third point.

Mistress Hutchinson is accused of claiming the revelation of God's Word directly to herself. That is, a Covenant of Grace.

ANNE: I have never—put it, Sir—claimed so in public.

WINTHROP: Before fifty to eighty women!

ANNE: In privacy, in my own house. Mr. Cotton has said that was allowed.

WINTHROP: I call witness, Mr. Bartholomew.

This was the Bartholomew whom Anne had known back in Alford and who had also been on the *Griffin*. His evidence was that Mistress Hutchinson had told him God divulged to her the exact day the ship would make landfall.

ANNE: And did it not?

WINTHROP: You have not the right to question, you are but to answer the statement, that you made testimony, in public, that God spoke to you directly.

ANNE: I was on board a ship, not yet in the public colony.

WINTHROP: There were naught but Puritan colonists there.

ANNE: But the Reverend Cotton, whose son Seaborn was born aboard the *Griffin*, the voyage previous, did not have his son baptized at sea, writing me saying it was not seemly. Not because he would have to use salt water, but that he was not on consecrated ground!

More appreciation from the throng; the bailiff pounded his kevel. Winthrop and Bartholomew put heads together. Then Bartholomew spoke further.

WITNESS: Please the Court, I knew Mistress Hutchinson in Alford. One day in a churchyard she did tell me God spoke to her of the death of two children in that one year, and so it happened.

WINTHROP: A churchyard is a public place.

ANNE: Sir, it is. Although there be mostly those that cannot hear.

WINTHROP: A public place!

ANNE: Put it, then, at that time I had not been warned against the Covenant of Grace.

WINTHROP: Bailiff. Any further disturbance Court shall be cleared.

Were they still on Point Three? She would keep on her feet, she could still stand.

WINTHROP: How do you know God revealed these things to you and not the Devil?

ANNE: I did not confess to either, in public. But how did Abraham know it was God's voice when He commanded him to sacrifice his only son, Isaac, and how did Abraham then know it was God's voice that stayed the knife?

WINTHROP: God spoke to the prophet Abraham and so He will speak straightaway with Mistress Hutchinson. . . . Repeat, you are not to ask questions.

Clearly the Deputy Governor was not getting the best of it. It seemed that he had lost the first two points. If he lost this point there was only one to go. Instead of this making him cautious it was having the opposite effect; how was his performance going down in front of the magistrates and, especially, Vane?

ANNE: God spoke not only to Abraham and Moses. He

spoke also to plain men, such as Job, and even to women—
Elizabeth, the sister of Mary, on the Birth, and to Sarah, the
barren wife—

WINTHROP: Enough. We weary of—

ANNE: But put it, sir, this is of such interest. You yourself
have called this New-England an Israel, a Promised Land,
and we Puritans as Hebrews, the Chosen of God . . .

WINTHROP: Not to the point.

VANE: Let her go on.

ANNE: Then. If God spoke direct to His Chosen, the Jews,
by this token, how can it be denied He speaks likewise to
Christians?

No answer in the record.

ANNE: Put it then, Christians are not *so* Chosen as—

WINTHROP: I call witness, Reverend Brother Symmes.

This was the minister who had been aboard the *Griffin*
along with Mr. Bartholomew, and had hastened ashore to protest Anne's admittance to the Church. Now he testified that
Anne had "preached" aboard the ship, to women.

WITNESS: These women have since become as young
branches sprung out of an old root, and there stands the
breeder and nourisher of all these distempers.

ANNE: May I answer?

VANE: She may.

ANNE: The young branches including the Reverend Brother
Symmes' own wife thanked me for my counsel, and I note
there are none here today of these tender limbs who would
speak out against me.

Winthrop had to ask Vane to call for silence. Anne must
have felt triumph, although she had just made a serious
blunder.

WINTHROP: Point Four . . .

But Anne was not ready to let go of Point Three. It had
been Mary Dyer's idea to use Winthrop's own statements

against him, and the two of them had labored on this at length.

Anne now humbly allowed as how she had read everything that the Deputy Governor had caused to have made public for "all our elucidation," and she would like to quote just two instances.

WINTHROP: Proceed, but be quick. *Tempus fugit.*

ANNE: Sir, I read of how one Archibald Thomson, carrying dung to his garden in a canoe in fair weather and still water, it sank under him in the harbor near shore and he was never seen after, because God was wroth for his working on the Sabbath.

WINTHROP: That is correct.

ANNE: And of how the ship *Mary Rolfe* blew up in the harbor with barrels of her own powder, because captain and crew had profaned God's name and laughed at protestors on the wharf, who were not harmed.

WINTHROP: Correct. What has this to do with Point Three?

ANNE: If you will refresh my memory—

WINTHROP: We are trying to establish your belief, that the Spirit of God can appear directly to anyone, without the interpretation of ministers.

ANNE: Yes. That is, Sir, it seems your own belief that God may give a sign most directly. His Word to Archibald Thomson and to the crew of the *Mary Rolfe* was immediate, they needed not wait for an interpretation by ministers of God's meaning through the Bible.

BAILIFF: Order.

Winthrop did not answer at once, and Anne must have felt emboldened. She suggested that perhaps the Court did not believe that the Spirit spoke directly to a common person in giving help or comfort, but only when His message was followed instantly by catastrophe.

ANNE: Put it, Sir, perhaps it is a case of either the Covenant of Grace, or of Dis-Grace.

BAILIFF: Order. Order!

If there was anything the spectators loved it was a pun or a play on words, especially when it pricked the importance of a religious concept they could never quite grasp.

Anne must have glanced across the bench at her dear Mr. Cotton, wondering if he were offended at her for making a pun on the Covenant of Grace. She must apologize for that.

WINTHROP: We will not be distracted by levity and disrespect. It has been claimed that you believe the Holy Spirit resides in yourself and everyone else. Therefore you need no ministers to interpret the Word of God. Therefore you would do away with the ministers. There follows you would then do away with this religious government. This is anarchy.

ANNE: I would not do away with all ministers. Some, such as— (She may have been about to mention the disgraced Wheelwright.) Mr. Cotton does preach very sweetly the Covenant of Grace.

WINTHROP: Mr. Cotton, Mr. Cotton. Have you told your Mr. Cotton—not in public, of course—that you as well as he are in a blessed state, the Covenant of Grace?

This must have startled Anne, and there was a pause. Winthrop did not hurry her. She tried hard to concentrate. What was it she had once told Mr. Cotton—*where* was it—in the churchyard?

ANNE: I member me now. I did tell Mr. Cotton of how it was, before my daughters were taken one after the other, God did give me a sign through His Word that this would happen.

WINTHROP: And what did Mr. Cotton say to that?

ANNE: He did say, why—that, yes, it was the role of ministers to interpret the Word but that—in times of great need perhaps the Spirit does speak direct.

WINTHROP: Thank you.

Anne must have stared at the Deputy Governor. Thank you!

WINTHROP: I call witness John Cotton. . . . You have heard the testimony last made by your communicant?

COTTON: Yes.

WINTHROP: Do you recall having made the statement she attests to you?

COTTON: No.

WINTHROP: Do you recall having made the statement attested, in any way, form or manner, changed about in words?

COTTON: No.

WINTHROP (to Anne): You are still lying, then, about the ministers, even your own, as will be proven more thoroughly in Point Four.

At this point John Cotton got up from the bench and left the room. This was not an unusual move; some three hours had passed, and magistrates and spectators were going in and out the doors to relieve themselves at the side of the court house or in the nearby fields.

What were Anne Hutchinson's thoughts now!

Without intermission, without a break for food, the proceedings went on. Point Four!

Anne, it was accused, had misrepresented the conduct of the ministers, and had stated at the time they came to her house, they were all, excepting Mr. Cotton, laboring under a Covenant of Works—and therefore preached nothing but forms and ceremony and had not the Spirit of God's Grace within them.

WINTHROP: Do you deny this?

ANNE: As God is my witness . . . I mean, as I am under oath . . . I did not say any such thing, at that time.

Had she? She remembered having told Mr. Cotton—was that before or after the ministers' visit?—that Mr. Wilson did so labor. . . . She repeated her denial.

Winthrop then brought forward several ministers who attested that she had claimed they "did so labor." One of these was Mr. Wilson. Anne denied them all, but faltered over Mr. Wilson.

WINTHROP: You recant here?

ANNE: I . . . did not speak against him at that time.

There was another putting together of heads, of murmuring all up and down the table. Suddenly, the points were over. And surely they had not proved a single basic accusation. Most important, she had not been tricked into asserting publicly her present belief in her own Covenant of Grace.

The short winter day was drawing into dusk, and from the bearable warmth of an earlier hour, it had gotten bitterly cold. Everyone was grumbling about it, as the doorman had not been able to replenish the burned-out coals in the foot warmers. Now the man went around drawing down from ceiling chains the iron and brass Betty lamps that resembled covered frying pans, and filled them with oil. No time out had been taken for rest or eating, and no one had offered Anne the opportunity either to sit down or go outside to perform a natural function. Pregnant, she had been standing some five hours. And now for the Errors . . . how many had they said? The ordeal was scarcely begun. She must have seen at that point that they meant to wear her down. And this must have given her some strength.

Error 36: No minister can preach the Covenant of Works without he be blessed with that of Grace. . . . This is contrary to the Scriptures [Bible reference given]. Anne watched lamplight that shone in nimbus halos, between them pockets of gloom. *Error 43* [given]: *This is Out of Order.* Outside, the sound of leaden rain. Did it not usually stop raining after dark, and not start? As from a distance Anne heard Winthrop's voice complaining that whenever she gave answers they could not be heard from beyond the second row. Later— or was that just after she had tried to raise her voice, she heard him say that since she was comparing herself to Daniel in the lion's den, by the sound of her she resembled Daniel less than the lion let loose upon him. . . . Laughter in the court, the sound of the kevel. . . . *Error 58: No minister can teach one who has the Spirit within, more than that which one already knows.* Would Mistress Hutchinson be that one who cannot be taught by the ministers? . . . *Error 59: The magistrates have not the right* . . .

Anne did not hear the rest of Error 59; she let herself sink to the floor.

From Winthrop's diary: Mistress H. went into a "Faint," this an Attempt to gain Pity and postpone the Course of Justice.

When Anne came to she had been put onto a chair. Over her head she heard grumblings.

"We shall perish of *la grippe* here." "We shall all die fasting."

The trial was "carried over until Midday morrow."

Anne found herself a bed in someone's house in New Town. Mary Dyer was at her side. Mary seemed beside herself with indignation. To have put a pregnant woman through such an ordeal, and lied about her as well!

"You must make that trimmer Cotton swear. Then see if he will not remember!"

Anne was too weary to consider this. She could only manage to say, it was possible he had forgotten a single sentence years and years ago. . . . Why, she herself could not remember what she had said about Mr. Wilson when the ministers came to her house . . .

Mary's voice was receding rapidly, but insisting. *Make the ministers swear.*

Next morning she felt better. And coming into the court, saw they were going to let her sit down. So they were being charitable to one about to be banished. She looked at the men before her on the bench. Winthrop looked pleased with himself. Mr. Cotton was not to be seen.

The trial began without preamble. Winthrop called the first of several new witnesses. Most of them Anne could not remember having spoken to. Years later the historian Ferdinando Gorges, grandson of the Ferdinando who was just then trying to break the charter, reported on the testimony of two of these men: " 'This little nimble-tongued woman said she could find the Book of Revelation so full o' ravishing joy that I should never have cause for sin so long as I live, as for her part she had attained it already.' " " 'Come along with me,' said my friend, 'I'll bring you to a woman that preaches better Gospell than any of your black-coates at the Ninneversity, a Woman of another kind of Spirit, who hath had many revelations of things to come, as for my part,' says he, 'I had rather hear such a one, without no study, than any of your learned Scollars.' " Delighted approval from the spectators at this gibe at "Harverd ninnies."

Winthrop still was not through with his witness-calling. He delivered a speech aimed at those women in the audience who had attended Anne's meetings. "I cite a favorite Author of Mistress Hutchinson's, St. Paul, in his Epistle to Timothy. 'Concerning false teachers . . . Refuse profane and old wives' fables . . . seducing spirits . . . doctrines of devils . . . speaking lies in hypocrisy . . . (You shall all have your) consciences seared with a hot iron.' " He then called for women to come up and repent their association with Mistress Hutchinson.

A small procession followed; most of them wept; most confessed she had tried to make them believe the Holy Spirit was within them, but now the scales were lifted from their eyes. The last witness was a close friend of Anne's, whose children she had nursed; but she probably was not surprised, as Ursula Cole was the wife of one of the ministers. She may even have smiled, in her hopelessness, when one of her young women testified in tears, but with perfect truth:

"She—she said she would as lief hear a cat meow as Elder Shepard preach. Or a dog bark as Mr. Wilson growl!"

Now Sir Henry Vane himself was asking her if there were any statement she would like to make, before the arrival of the verdict. The verdict! She was in a panic; she said, yes, she would like to have the ministers sworn in.

This was unheard of; one can imagine the stir in the room. But Vane consented; and one by one they stood before the great Bible and were sworn. Then Anne repeated her avowal of the day before, that she had not accused them of preaching only a Covenant of Works at the time of their visit. One by one they insisted she had. Suddenly there was Mr. John Cotton. He gave testimony calmly. He said he did not remember that Mistress Hutchinson had said that any of them did so labor, at this time, and he would swear this ten times over.

With Cotton's positive statement, the trial was over.

To deliver the verdict, Sir Henry Vane got to his feet, and motioned to Anne to do likewise.

In view of the evidence presented by Deputy Governor Winthrop (said Vane), his magistrates, all ministers giving witness, and all other divers witnesses, this Religious Court finds no reason for banishment of the accused, or even for severe censure. The Court contents itself with abjuring Mistress Hutchinson from holding further meetings of women at her house. The Court is hereby adjourned.

Shouts, cheers, applause. Mary Dyer rushed up and embraced Anne. Captain Underhill and Mr. Coddington came around from the bench and clasped her hand. Will Hutchinson wept with relief. It was all over, the nightmare was at an end!

And Anne? Once she had gotten over the first wave of

disbelief—was she asleep and dreaming?—all her confidence of the day before came flooding back to sustain her. Of course! Hadn't she taken the wind out of every sail that Winthrop had hoisted?

And hadn't she been shown a sign that she would prevail?

The open Bible on the bench—The Sermon on the Mount. "Blessed are they which are persecuted for righteousness' sake; for theirs is the Kingdom of Heaven."

In triumph, Anne turned to the person nearest her, ex-Governor John Winthrop.

"I knew I would be saved!" she exclaimed. God had given her a sign as she stood on this very spot—from the Bible on which she had sworn!

In the absolute silence that followed, it could not have taken her more than an instant to realize what she had said. She had claimed, in the most public place of all, to have received the Holy Spirit, direct.

And now it was impossible for the Court to let her go. Within the hour, Governor Vane announced that having put the matter of banishment to a vote: "Yea-sayers being the Deputy Governor, all Magistrates and Ministers with Except, one. Nay-sayers being I, Henry Vane, William Coddington, John Underhill, John Cotton."

Mistress Hutchinson therefore was "suspended," and her person should be given over into the care of a certain worthy of Roxbury Town, upon the posting of a forty-pound bond, where she should be "confined til the season of the year might be fit and fair for her banishment. This Court is dismissed."

Entry in diary of John Winthrop:
"3 Nov. 1637. She talked to her own hurt."

UNEASY INTERLUDE

Anne was supposed to be in Coventry, that is, no one was to be talking to her until the passing of her sentence. Actually, everybody was. That winter, the house of Joseph Weld, wealthiest Puritan in the colony, was in a continual state of excitement. Anne's younger children clung to her, frightened and bewildered. Her husband came and went, looking for a farm outside the colony, along Narragansett Bay. The ministers came with a prepared paper of recantation—all she had to do was to admit that she had never had any direct signs from the Holy Spirit, and all would be forgiven. She would not sign the paper; it would not be right to deny God's voice. John Cotton came, avowing that he had truly forgotten that little scene in the churchyard at Alford so many years ago, and so dare not perjure himself before God. Anne said it did not matter.

To Henry Vane she confessed, "I am so troubled that I cannot speak. Will the Lord cast me off forever?" During the long months she kept asking, "Has God forgotten to be gracious? Is His mercy clean gone?"

And Vane kept assuring her there was still hope. Official banishment would not come before the first of April. Plenty of time for him, Coddington, and Underhill, yes, and even Cotton, to go to work on the magistrates. And in his best lighthearted manner the young governor quoted Sir Thomas More, beheaded by Henry VIII: "All martyrs succeed in infuriating their executioners!"

Also coming to the house was Mary Dyer. According to her, Cotton would be relieved if she were banished, to exonerate himself from any "taint" of her. Anne said she did not want to hear anything more.

She had still other visitors—Indian women whose children she had nursed. They could not understand what had happened to her except that it had something to do with her god.

Strange, when they knew that *God* paid them no attention at all. He was too busy chasing, but never catching, the goddess who lived in the Moon!

And there were two young men, John Throgmorton and Thomas Cornell, who visited Anne. They had scarcely heard of Mistress Hutchinson before the trial, but now they pledged their wholehearted support of her, if there was anything they could do, and with their families behind them.

And so in that winter Vane was working on the magistrates in Anne's behalf—and Winthrop on the ministers—to keep badgering her. The governor wrote: "She is still talking to her own hurt. The difference between the official belief and her own is as great as heaven and hell."

The ministers' harassment served not to change Anne's beliefs but to bring up even more ways in which hers were not in accordance with the Puritanical. Under their goading she said finally that "You should not sanction the selling of numbers of Indian boys and women as slaves, rejoycing in the Church at good sales, since on one hand you preach the people whatever skin are all of one blood, on the other, these are not human because they are not in Christ."

And: "All ceremonies are wrong. You have cast out the Cross in baptism, but you should cast off baptism itself, the child knows not what is being done to him in his name." "As for the Sacrament of the Lord's Supper (Communion), to make use of bread, or the juice of a Silly Grape to represent the Body and Blood of Christ, it is as bad as Necromancy to perform it."

Necromancy—black magic!

WINTHROP: This American Jezebel hath truly the Devil in her. She has held those meetings like a Witch's coven. These wise and faithful ministers have found her out, she with her familiar, Dyer, who would soon have driven Christ and Gospel out of New England. Now they shall all be rooted out.

There is no doubt that Winthrop, by then at least, believed Anne Hutchinson had been sent to him straight from Satan, and that if he did not rid the colony of her, it would be forsaken by God.

The date was 15 March, 1638.

WINTHROP: "At this time the good providence of God arranged it so that several of the congregation were away, among them Mistress Hutchinson's husband. Also Wm. Coddington, gone south to see relatives. . . . Underhill is again engaged with the salvages." Winthrop picked then to strike.

VERDICT

On the 15th, after the usual Thursday religious lecture, at ten in the morning, Anne was rushed to the court without an hour to prepare herself. This second trial lasted as long as the first, with the same conditions—no rest, no food, no heat. Anne behaved so as to make more than one reporter of the event admit that she probably was possessed of the Devil. Five months pregnant, she refused a chair and stood the whole time. She not only refused to take back her latest "Errors," she added to them. "Sunday should not be set aside as the Lord's Day, we should be good Christians every day." "You should not preach we will have these same bodies in heaven. What of men who have been burned? We shall put on new bodies."

She even managed to tempt Sir Henry Vane to turn against her by bringing up the "lies and slander" she and Mary Dyer had suffered at the rumor that the governor had been the father of both her dead child and "the monster"—when this rumor had all but died away!

Finally, the vote among the officials. It was thirty to one for banishment. Before sentence could be passed, Anne threw herself on the mercy of the Court. "I am no Puritan, I see now, so I will leave the Church, but let me stay where I belong."

This could not be, said Winthrop. "As the admission of a member is by consent of the whole, so must be his dismissal. God is not the author of confusion. If one member may depart, why may not ten, yea, an hundred, the minister himself leave his people, or all of them leave him?" Thus the Puritan logic.

Anne began to shout. "Take heed what you go about to do to me. You have no power over my body and if you do me harm God will ruin you, and your posterity, and this whole state and this religion."

"She has cursed us," said Winthrop. Anne began to shout at the magistrates and ministers. The courtroom was thrown into turmoil. In the midst of the confusion young John Throgmorton and Thomas Cornell rushed to Anne's side, and despite the screams of their families, were promptly banished along with her. The official speech of "casting out," which, as Anne's senior minister, was the duty of the Reverend Wilson to deliver, began:

"In the name of the Lord Jesus Christ and in the name of the church I do not only pronounce you worthy to be cast out, but I do cast you out; and in the name of Christ I do deliver you up to Satan, that you may learn no more to blaspheme, to seduce, and to lie; and I do account you from this time forth to be a Heathen and a Publican, and so to be held of all the brethern and sisters of this congregation and of others: therefore I command you in the name of Christ Jesus and of this church as a leper to withdraw yourself out of the congregation."

Anne heard this terrible pronouncement without any comment. And then it was the turn of her own minister, John Cotton, to make the verdict official. He stood and, after referring briefly to some notes, began:

"The great questions of this present time are how far liberty of conscience ought to be given to these that truly fear God? And how far restrained to turbulent persons that not only raze the foundation of godliness, but disturb the civil peace! I now cite freely from Isaiah 16. . . ." Anne began to cry aloud at him, but he went ahead. " 'We have heard of the pride of Moab, even of his haughtiness, but his boasts are false. . . . Send ye therefore the lamb to the ruler of the land . . . to execute judgment . . .' " The shrill voice of the hysterical woman keened across the droning, memorized notes of the minister. " 'For it shall be as a wandering bird is cast out of the nest, so will be the sons and daughters of Moab . . . into the wilderness. . . . Hide the outcasts; betray not him that wandereth. . . . Make thy shadow as the night in the midst of noonday. . . . Let everyone wail for Moab, everyone mourn. . . . I will bewail with weeping for this vine that has been cut off. I will water thee with my tears. For thy harvest is fallen. Gladness and joy are taken away. My soul moans like a lyre. My bowels sound like an harp.' " Anne Hutchinson collapsed.

A historian of the time happened to make an unimportant observation. He noted:

"Tears stood in the eyes of Sir Henry Vane."

REVERBERATIONS

Immediately after the trial, new elections were held. John Winthrop was again elected governor; and for their parts in defending, or not attacking, Anne Hutchinson, he and his magistrates condemned to be banished her brother-in-law John Wheelwright, Captain John Underhill, William Coddington, and Sir Henry Vane.

John Winthrop went on to serve a total of eleven terms as governor, until his death.

Sir Henry Vane, forced to return to England, resumed his

political career at court, where, at the age of forty-nine, he was accused of treason (historians say falsely), and he who had quoted Sir Thomas More to Anne Hutchinson was himself beheaded in the Tower of London.

Captain Underhill took himself and his family to a wild area of Connecticut and, along with two others who had sympathized with Anne (Robert Feakes and Daniel Patrick), helped settle the town of Greenwich.

John Wheelwright went north to the New Hampshire territory and founded the town of Exeter.

William Coddington joined another, earlier, outcast, Roger Williams, in Providence, the town Williams had settled. There they were joined by Anne Hutchinson and her family, Mary Dyer, and eighteen others from the Massachusetts Bay Colony.

Indians, both savage and friendly, abounded in the Providence area, but also there were many Quakers and Baptists, and so Anne and her friends settled on an island in Narragansett Bay called Rhodes. While a simple frame house was being built, Anne and the others lived for protection, as was usual in wild areas, in a dug-out pit in the ground, the earth walls cased with tree bark, the floor with planks. And thus began the town of Portsmouth.

Then Anne had a falling-out with Coddington; a Quaker, he believed in no ministers at all. In a friendly enough parting, Coddington left, and began building a town at the southern tip of the island, which he called Newport.

On June 11, 1638, an earthquake shook the area that was later to be known as Rhode Island, while Anne was preaching her Covenant of Grace, and she was nearly killed. Hearing of this back in Boston, Governor Winthrop wrote that the quake showed "God's continued disquietude against the existence of Anne Hutchinson, now living with her Witch's coven on the Isle of Errors."

In August, Anne gave birth. The child was stillborn.

On September 12, 1641, "a great tempest-like hurricane" lashed over the land, and the roof of Anne's house was blown off.

In the spring of 1642, Will Hutchinson died. Hearing of this, Winthrop sent a delegation of ministers to Portsmouth, among them Mr. John Wilson. Spokesman for the group, Mr. Wilson informed Anne the jurisdiction of Massachusetts would soon be extended to take in both Exeter, where Wheelwright was again preaching, and Portsmouth; and so even at this late date they had better both recant. Quakers and Baptists who ventured into Boston were having their ears cut off; a woman had been pressed to death "to stop her lying breath," and a minister named Abrahams, "whose children should have been baptized, was thrown bodily from the pulpit into the street."

Anne got word to Wheelwright, who fled to Maine. For herself and her group, they went down to an area a bit south of Greenwich where, along with Captain Underhill, the Throgmorton and Cornell families had also settled.

Here, however, the two families reported the Indians were ominously restive, and they were considering moving once more. Underhill had "gone to fight them up the North river at Sing-Sing" (Algonkin for Rock on Rock). There was a house to be had nearby, but they would not recommend taking it at this time.

Anne and her family rented a boat and sailed around the area. At the tip of the Long Island they found a new community called Gravesend being built, and went ashore to be greeted by its leader, Lady Deborah Moody. Lady Moody showed them around the bright new town where, she said, complete religious freedom had been written into the charter. That certainly appealed to Anne Hutchinson, and she asked about land for sale. Lady Moody said there was just one plot available; she, as founder, had taken for herself two plots; Mistress Hutchinson might have the second.

But Anne did not want to be separated from her group, so she declined, saying she would probably settle in the area known as Hell Gate. Lady Moody advised against this, saying that Indians were thick around there and all complaining to the Dutch governor about white settlers camped on lands that had not been paid for.

But Anne left with her thanks, saying she had never had any trouble with Indians. And so, in June or July, 1643, she moved into a house near the Throgmortons and Cornells, to await Underhill's return.

Her neighbors, alarmed that she would not keep firearms, persuaded her to accept a few of the big hounds they themselves kept around the grounds. Anne took the dogs, but most of the time they remained tied up, since she was soon making friends among the Indians. At first they had skulked around the house, curious to take the measure of this new white family on what no doubt they felt was their land. But Anne showed no fear; she beckoned the squaws to come see her new kitchen, with its artesian well right outside the door. This was oohed and grunted at. And she drew water for the braves who had been out on all-day deer hunts. After the years of stormy dissension with her own kind, it felt strangely comforting to be among these uncritical, unchristianized darkskins! Anne liked their childlike curiosity, and perhaps even envied them somewhat their more carefree style of living.

But there was one aspect of the Indian character about which Anne Hutchinson knew nothing. And that was the fact that young Indian braves often burn with the desire to cover themselves with individual glory, to prove their valor and importance in the sight of their peers and the tribe. Such a brave was Wampage.

Wampage lived just across the creek that ran by the Hutchinson house, in a Siwanoy village among the cornfields of Laap-ha-wach-king (now Pelham or Eastchester). And Wampage was itching with urge to distinguish himself, at the same time ridding his people of the white intruders upon their homelands and hunting grounds. Now he rounded up five or six other braves and, with native craftiness, planned a surprise attack on the three houses along the banks of a narrow stream, each separated by a stretch of woodland. On the morning of the day agreed on—most accounts give it as August 20—the little band took stock of the situation at each home. Then they returned at dusk.

They struck first at the settlement of Thomas Cornell. Cornell's fierce pack of hounds took some toll, but in minutes they were all hacked or clubbed to death. Then to the rage of the marauders they discovered that the entire family was absent—only three or four farm laborers were at work in the barn and stables. The Indians set fire to everything, burning the horses and cattle alive. Whooping and hollering, they proceeded eastward to the next homestead.

Young John Throgmorton had time to grab up a gun, and his rapid fire kept the savages at bay while the rest of his family fled out the back and into their rowboat. Then young John was killed and scalped.

Rowing frantically up the creek, the Throgmortons heard the shouts and screams, crackle and roar of flames destroying their new house and barns. But their only thought was to reach the next house in line, and warn the Hutchinsons of the approach of the murderous gang.

The landing place was a quarter mile upstream past the Hutchinsons'. As they came alongside the house they knew they were already too late.

On that summer evening, Anne was at home with her younger children—Francis, about 21, William, 12, Anne about 18, and William Collins, young Anne's husband, with the girls, Mary, Katherine, and Susannah, at age nine the youngest. Also at home were a house servant and a field hand.

Somebody heard, a way down the creek, the sounds of fighting. But nobody took alarm; the Indians in the nearby villages were always stirring up some excitement among themselves.

A little later, the Hutchinson dogs started up, barking wildly. Anne came out on the porch, to find a knot of Indians at the gate. They signaled her for water, as they so often did. And would she tie up her snapping dogs? Anne called to her children to come and help her do this.

When the dogs were all securely tied, the Indians struck. The one survivor of the massacre that followed—the child Susannah—could not remember in the ensuing horror how her mother was killed. It is only to be hoped that Anne was quickly dispatched and did not live to witness the slaying of her family. Amid the screams and shouts, the howling of the helpless dogs, the house and barn were set afire; and Katherine, seeking to escape over the fence, was dragged back by her long hair to a tree stump, where her head was hacked off. Somehow in the carnage little Susannah was snatched up and spared—to be carried off by the triumphant band.

Later that evening, the Throgmortons, grieving for their slain and mutilated son, came upon the grisly scene. And then made their grim report to others.

Governor Winthrop was not just vindicated, he was impressed; he had never before heard of Indians wiping out a whole family: "God's hand is apparently seen herein, to pick out this woful woman, to make her . . . an unheard-of heavy example. . . . Appropriate that the massacre took place at this 'Hell Gate.' Proud Jezebel has at last been cast down."

Others did not agree with the governor. From all over New England came bitter accusations. "Your cruel Dealings with Anne Hutchinson, and those others, stands as a perpetual Record before the Lord against you—the Guilt and Weight of whose Blood lyes upon you as if done by you." "The next piece of wickedness I am to mind you of is your barbarous action committed against Mistress Hutchinson, whom you at first imprisoned, then banished, and so exposed her to that desolate condition that she fell into the hands of the Indians, who murdered her and her family . . ."

Her contemporaries saw Anne Hutchinson as a victim of religious intolerance. A later century was to see as more positive the part she played in history. Her banishment, coming on the heels of that of Roger Williams', awakened even greater awareness in New Englanders of the need to break out of the formalism that was gripping their lives; and her joining forces with Williams, that champion of democracy, led to the first of many quickenings in the direction of freedom of speech that culminated in the separation of church and state that in most areas of the country is taken for granted today. It is sad but true that such tragic and dramatic events as those that happened to Anne Hutchinson are usually needed before wresting a change from things-as-they-are.

In 1643, when Anne died, there was no funeral eulogy delivered over the pitiful remains. In 1652, when her minister, John Cotton, died, his senior, John Wilson, orated over his coffin, calling him "a learned, judicious, reverend, holy, goodly, worthy, pious, divine and faithful servant." Anne Hutchinson's trial had made Cotton so famous that the next generation of New England women named their babies after him. Cotton's own grandson was Increase Mather, his great-grandson, Cotton Mather, both minister-judges at the witch trials that were to terrorize Salem in 1692.

Anne Hutchinson, too, left her name in many ways and places. The stream upon whose banks she was killed was given the name Hutchinson; today it has dwindled to a trickle, and hidden at that; but above it runs a macadam road known as the Hutchinson River Parkway. (The place where John Throgmorton was killed is now a sailboat harbor known as Throgs Neck.)

Perhaps the strangest way in which Anne's name survived

was that her murderer took it for his own. The Indian Wampage derived considerable importance from his savage exploit. And so he took the name of his victim, and was known thereafter as Ann-houck; and his village itself became known to the English as Anne's Hook.

And what of that surviving Hutchinson, Susannah? The child lived with her Indian "rescuers" for four years, and then was ransomed by the Dutch. She wrote later that despite her still-vivid memories of the massacre, she had not been unhappy growing up with Indian children, and she parted from her foster family with reluctance. On December 30, 1651, Susannah married John Cole of Rhode Island, the son of Ursula Cole who had been forced to give evidence against Anne at the trial.

The death of Anne Hutchinson set off yet another chain of events. Captain John Underhill, back from his skirmish with the Indians upriver at Sing-Sing and hearing of the massacre of the Hutchinsons and young Throgmorton—the friends who had moved there to be near his protection—was seized with rage and the thirst for revenge. He went out with his men and raided and burned whole Siwanoy villages; upwards of two hundred and fifty men, women, and children were slain; a hundred bodies were collected and heaped on a hilltop. The Indians retaliated by surging together in a far-flung revolt that was to be known as the Three-Year War. It was this war, begun in late 1643, which would now force the entire town of Gravesend to flee for its life.

Part III

OF BUILDING

11

A Steeple Without a Church

Q: When is a town wall not a town wall?
A: When the natives have worn paths through the holes in it.

This was a local joke going around the unfinished town of Gravesend in December of 1643. Additional observations were directed at the town hall, roofless, and the church, where Lady Deborah Moody planned to have Penelope van Princes and Richard Stout marry, as soon as it got a steeple on it.

She was still trying to finish whitewashing her kitchen that morning when she got the surprise of her life—an Indian at the Dutch door. This was nothing in itself; despite the continual mischiefs they were still allowed to come and go because of the value of their barter, and so long as they did not carry guns. But this Indian, tall and fierce as he was, spoke to Lady Deborah in English. She was so disarmed, she unlatched the bottom half of the door and invited him to step in.

And so, a few moments later, when Penelope came into the kitchen for breakfast, there was Tisquantum scowling at her!

Penelope was terrified, remembering the scene of torture she had witnessed, and that runaways got their throats cut—and *she* had run away with a canoe. But the old chief only grunted his disgust. The canoe had been found overturned in midstream the following day; she would never have made a good squaw! He was here for a serious reason.

He had paddled over to the town out of curiosity to see if she was there, had spied her and was about to leave when he overheard some other "men" talking of the treachery committed by a captain of the Dutch; this captain had raided innocent, peaceable camps in the night and slaughtered braves, squaws, and babies in their sleep, then had thrown their bodies on the brow of a hill. And this meant all-out war. "They—burn you all down." And he, Tisquantum, was taking a mortal risk in warning the white one, the little Wahpayweepit, because they had walked and talked the "Yangeese" together. For any other white skins he cared not, he finished; and stalked out in his weathered dignity.

Lady Deborah was faced with her first major decision in the short life of the community. To make it, she called a town meeting—the first—in the roofless town hall. She told everybody assembled the news the Indian had brought. Should they stay or leave?

Captain Richard Stout spoke for the majority of the guards: Stay! Nobody trusted the word of an Indian; this must be a trick to make the whites flee so that they could get in and burn down the town. Somebody else stood up and reminded them all of the recent terrible sweep of killings and burnings at Hell Gate, where the Hutchinson family had been wiped out. That certainly boded ill for a peaceful winter. The discussion grew general and out of it came—Why not leave the men here to defend the town in case of attack, and send the women and children to New Amsterdam to the relative safety of the fort?

The matter was put to a vote. The result, a tie. Lady Deborah would have to decide, after all, by herself. Why had she ever thought she would enjoy the responsibility of running a town in the middle of nowhere?

About that first decision she was later to write a friend: "After I gave it none of the men moved, until they saw their wives hurrying off to gather up the children." (Women leaders don't give the same kind of order as men.) What Lady Deborah had said was,

"I think that, since discretion is the better part of valor—"

As it developed, they had not a quarter hour to spare. Indian canoes could be seen approaching as Richard Stout halloed the only vessel within hailing distance, a fodder boat. Its deck was taken up almost entirely with a huge bale of hay; but there would be room around the rails.

Before they were out of sight of the town, they heard gunfire from shore and saw the first flame-tipped arrows winging in. The men of the boat crew began hoisting more sail, alarmed about their cargo of tinder-dry winter hay. As the boat tacked around the point of land, Lady Deborah leaned over the rail for a last look at her burning town, then said a prayer for the safety of the men. Especially for seventeen-year-old Sir-Harry, whose first battle this would be. And for Richard Stout; Lady Deborah glanced down the railing to where Penelope too was straining for one more look. Poor young widow, she must be wondering if she is going to lose a second man before she even walks him down the aisle!

Next day the Indians were trying to burn down New Amsterdam. They didn't succeed, at least in part because of Lady Deborah's warning. All ships in the encircling harbor were alerted to train their guns on any Indian canoes approaching. Despite this, one band of marauders was able to sneak ashore; they headed straight for the Dutch West India settlement and were driven off with difficulty, Director General Kieft having to fly down Heere Street with his head alongside the neck of his horse. Apparently the Indians blamed the latest atrocity of those bodies heaped on the hilltop on the Dutchman they hated so much.

Most of the townspeople had been sheltered behind the earthwork walls of the fort, and there Lady Deborah renewed her acquaintance with Nicholas Stillwell, the representative of the Dutch West India Company who, on a calmer occasion the year before, had shown her around the city. Stillwell as usual was blaming this new uprising on Kieft, "the most unparalleled scoundrel ever to disgrace a colonial outpost's authority"; and he, Stillwell, not being Dutch himself, could not lift a finger to get him removed. It was never to occur to Englishmen like Stillwell—during the raids, burning, and bloodshed of the next three years—that to blame the Dutch for everything was a case of the pot calling the kettle black.

On the following day the men of Gravesend trooped wearily into the fort. The Indians had left them little to defend, so they were throwing in their lot with the Dutch. Lady Deborah held herself back from embracing a grimy but unharmed Sir-Harry; Penelope van Princes observed no such restraint toward Richard Stout.

The young couple were married next day, New Year's, in the small church within the walls of the fort. Willem Kieft performed the Dutch Lutheran ceremony, the congregation of townspeople was more than half Dutch, a windmill loomed in the foreground, and for the wedding feast Kieft had had a pig slaughtered, served up with curries and chutneys; it was more than a girl from far-off Amsterdam had any right to expect.

The general said his men had managed to bring down from his bouwerie enough ham on the hoof and hogsheads of West India rum to see everyone happily through an Indian siege. The "siege," however, was not to materialize. The Indians had burned, looted, and moved on, at least for the time being; cautiously, townsmen and Gravesend refugees emerged. Penelope Stout made a beeline for the windmill, her new husband racing to catch up with her. The Dutch girl embarked on an immediate effort to bring her ignorant Englishman up to date on everything superiorly Dutch; for instance, did he know the sails of a windmill could be set to catch the wind from any direction, and that during the Religious Wars, Hollanders used them to pass coded messages across the dykes and far out to sea? And did *she* know, said Richard Stout, that a windmill filled with flour sacks looked like a very private and interesting place for a honeymoon?

It was too soon to venture returning to Gravesend, so Lady Deborah played guide to Sir-Harry in her second walk-around tour of the town. The usually teeming marketplace was deserted because of the raid, and most of the shops were shut up; but one tavern keeper was just then opening for business again. Lady Deborah's practiced eye for real estate had picked out his swinging sign as one put up since she'd been there last. It depicted a soldier on a wooden horse holding a pitcher in one hand and a short sword in the other. There was something amazingly familiar about that pose! Just then the tavern keeper spotted the two and called out their names. Then Lady Deborah recognized the man as Philip Geraerdy, the guard she had been obliged to discipline for having gotten drunk on duty. He had been made to "ride" a wooden horse in the Gravesend parade carrying a pitcher and sword to show he loved beer better than battle. And now, with defiant good humor, he had opened a tavern and named it "The Wooden Horse"! The cheerful innkeeper invited his former employer inside for a refreshing beaker of ale.

By the time they had walked around the island and come back to the fort, Lady Deborah, self-educated authority on town planning and development, felt the need to sum up her opinion of the future of New Amsterdam. "A pity about the place," she said to Sir-Harry. It boasted such a deep magnificent harbor, yet its land area was so small and rocky, there was "nowhere to expand." Otherwise, it might have grown into a seaport as great, say, as Liverpool!

*

Two days later the settlers sailed back to Gravesend—on the Bruijkleen ferry. Since there was no ferryboat man, everybody wanted Lady Deborah to take the tiller, but she insisted that this was the work of a man, and gave it over to Captain Richard Stout. Then she moved around the boat, insisting with some jocularity that all pay the required three stuyvers. Being raided, did this not always cost money? There was much joking as the little party drew near their ruined town. On coming ashore, however, the joking died away, as they surveyed the loss of their efforts and the enormity of the task that lay ahead.

And then they came upon an incongruous sight. Next to the ruined church, in a sandpit, lay the unharmed steeple, awaiting its hoisting to a now nonexistent roof. Everybody stood around, gloomily contemplating this useless object. Then one man glanced at another, and suddenly a dozen of them were leaping into the shallow pit. Brawny arms seized the ungainly cone and began pushing and heaving at it. In an instant the rest of the assembly had caught on; children jumped down with cries of excitement, the women following with encouraging shouts. Slowly the steeple rose until it stood erect, the cross at the top now high above their heads.

Everyone gave a cheer. And then grew quiet.

After a moment, Lady Deborah's voice rose in the clear air.

"Our Father which art in heaven, Hallowed be thy name."

The murmur of a hundred others joined in. "Thy kingdom come. Thy will be done in earth, as it is in heaven.

"Give us this day our daily bread.

"And forgive us our debts, as we forgive our debtors.

"And lead us not into temptation, but deliver us from evil:

"For thine is the kingdom, and the power, and the glory, for ever. Amen."

The service was over. The rebuilding could begin.

12

The Grande Dame of Gravesend

". . . And two brass candlesticks, each for two candles, be pleased to send me ones that slide up and down, according to the new style."

There was one benefit in being obliged to refurnish one's home practically from scratch, Lady Deborah reflected. You could take advantage of the new styles! Of course there were a great many objects she would be ordering in very much the old style; she was writing her ordering letters at a desk—only slightly charred from the fire—that would one day be called a "Governor Winthrop," but her favorite styles in furniture were the antiques of the 1600s, which combined elaborate carvings with long graceful lines and were known as "Flam-buoyant Gothic" and "Late Perpendicular." She was ordering chests of drawers, wardrobes, and dish cabinets of these, as well as "another harpsichord, and if any are a new style so as to be fire-withstanding, be pleased to send such a one."

At least most of the domestic equipment had escaped, the

copper, leather-bound milk cans, stoneware oil and wine jars, brass lamps whose clamp held a slender rush that made delicate Japanese-like shadows on Lady Deborah's white walls. Yes, and those absolute necessities, the brass bed-warming pans that she passed through cold damp sheets before daring to slip between them. Oh, but how she was going to miss, for the rest of the winter, her porcelain floor-vase. Beautifully painted, it had stood about a foot high, on rollers, with handles at the sides for moving it about. One put live coals in the vase, sat in a chair and wheeled the vase under one's long, full skirts. In 1644 this was indeed central heating!

And Lady Deborah ordered books. Several new Bibles, but also "anything you think will add to our woful lack of culture here." (The result was a thin but steady stream of books from Europe over the next ten years, and in Lady Deborah's having the largest library in the province of New Amsterdam —some two hundred volumes.)

Praise to Providence, the pair of silver salt cellars, heirlooms with the Moody initials, had escaped—six-sided and standing proud as chessmen, with a scene engraved on each side of the pair depicting a month of the year. Lady Deborah would willingly live in a wilderness, but if she could not have had her salt cellars to hand down to her son when he married—!

She was enjoying a new occupation, that of cooking; back on her English estate she had done little besides give orders to her cooks. There was a satisfying, earthy goodness in cooking a venison stew (*bouilli*) in an iron pot suspended from chains over the fireplace. And happily she crushed peppercorns, nutmeg, and cinnamon with mortar and pestle, sliced pieces off the sugar loaf with the sugar cutter, and the salt loaf *ditto* with the salt saw, which had a bronze, nonrusting blade. She left the supervision of the roasting to Sir-Harry, enjoying the wonderful smells that filled the house as he turned the joint of pig or goose on the iron spit with its drip pan below to catch the fat that would later be made into soap.

It was probably at Gravesend that the expression was coined, "With the pig nothing is wasted but the squeal."

There was great variety for the taking around Gravesend, even with a sporadic war going on. The waters teemed with oysters, lobsters, sturgeon, and salmon, so plentiful they couldn't be sold for a penny. The air yielded geese, duck, and pigeons; the fields produced (without years off) corn and pumpkins, squash and beans, and flax for the making of linen clothes. In the woods, where hunters now went heavily armed, besides trees bearing plums, cherries, and peaches, there were deer, beaver, and lynx, coney, hogs, and bears, and the wild turkey, though the men agreed it took the fleeter-footed Indian to catch them. And walnut trees for their nuts and beautiful wood, and magnolias, two of which Lady Deborah had replanted in her garden—along with flowers that provided domestic benefit, such as the soapwort: its pink-white petals were ignored; the roots and stems were used in washing clothes. However, since soapwort turned white material reddish, there were few pure white washes spread out on the grass in Gravesend. Because of all the lavish providence supplied by Nature, a poet in New Amsterdam wrote, "A Land heaped with Blessings Kind . . . a Land where Milk and Honey flows, a Very Eden." By "land" the poet meant all of New Netherland; and in another verse he reflected it was a pity that with such *largesse* some people could still not be happy in this blessed place!

In her "ordering" bout, Lady Deborah engaged the services of nimble-fingered Penelope Stout to make her a few more of the blue and dark-red velvet dresses, with wide white collars, that were then the fashion. Penelope had appointed herself the town seamstress. The other "professions" were carpenter, wood sawyer, tailor, baker, chimney sweep, cooper, mason, miller, surgeon, butcher, and the schoolteacher, who doubled as gravedigger, probably because his work was physically the lightest. The only ready food that could be bought was at the baker's—and at that, most women were proud to turn out their own baking. Not Lady Deborah, who went daily to the fragrant-smelling shop. She knew she was a failure at turning corn meal into light delicious cakes and might better occupy her time designing a good drainage system. Everyone should do what he could do best!

Lady Deborah found that she was quite good at making "hornbooks" for helping children learn their ABCs. These were pages on which had been written the alphabet; the page was backed by a thin piece of wood and covered for protection with a transparent amber-colored slice of animal horn. Until the schoolhouse was finished Lady Deborah held classes in her back parlor and handed out hornbooks on which she had also inscribed such verses as:

> In Adam's Fall
> We sinned all.
>
> Xerxes did die
> And so must I.
>
> Our days begin with trouble here
> Our life is but a span
> And cruel death is always near
> So frail a thing is man.

These were the sentiments that sprang naturally to the English mind of the 1600s even though their inscriber might not be in the least gloomy. Lady Deborah's "readers" were far from gloomy, either, even in those first years when the Indian wars prevented them from running freely and exploring wherever they liked. They learned from Lady Deborah how to make dolls from cornhusks, using the floppy silk as hair; and magic lanterns from cloth stretched around boxes—these projected pictures on the wall; and how to sing in chorus. Lady Deborah well remembered from England the "waits," strolling bands of chimney sweeps who sang carols to the accompaniment of horn-blowing and the sweet clatter of coins tossed out of windows. And did not the Bible itself say, in Psalm 100, "Make a joyful noise unto God, all ye lands, sing forth the honor of his name"?

Well, then, there should be singing at Gravesend. And so the Christmas ceremonies of 1644 included a semicircle of cherubim gathered at the steeple in the sandpit, singing the madrigals of William Byrd and Thomas Tallis, such as "Greensleeves," and carols like "God Rest Ye Merrie, Gentlemen, Let Nothing You Dismay."

In spring the books began to arrive. Everybody wanted to borrow them—the women, especially, pored over the poetry selections for inspiration for the cross-stitched samplers that were framed and hung in every kitchen. One of the favorites was by an Edward Taylor. It was a rather unusual choice in an era when most samplers read, "God Bless This House." But the people of Gravesend had just set aside a grassy plot for a bowling green, on which they rolled balls in communal sport, and here was a chance to combine their love of God with their pleasure in life. The most popular quotation, therefore, that went up on the walls, usually with a stylized and smiling yellow orb, looked most un-Puritan:

"Who in This Bowling Alley Bowled the Sun?"

By summer 1645, the skirmishes between Indians and Dutch, English and Indians, and French and anybody they happened to encounter had moved away from the Bruijkleen area toward both Long Island and New Jersey, leaving Lady Deborah to visit her pig farm! The pigs were kept, under armed guard, on a five-mile spit of land adjacent to Gravesend, an area which boasted exceptionally fine white sand. The Indian wars might drag on, but Lady Deborah considered it a hardship to do without a weekend's roast of pig, *and* sea-scrubbed sand every day to scatter on her fine wood floors.

And so she set forth with Penelope Stout for company, accompanied by Richard Stout and Sir-Harry. The way to this spit was across a creek; Stout and his fellow guards had filled in a section at the narrowest part with a path built of oyster and clam shells. Lady Deborah observed every time she crossed this path that the Indians were steadily chipping away at the clamshells which they valued in the making of wampum-peak. And so, she reflected, would she be chipping away at a path if it were paved with shillings and sixpence!

Sir-Harry, Lady Deborah knew, wasn't along so much to protect his mother as in hopes of digging up a treasure chest reportedly buried by some pirate ship's crew. Sir-Harry had recently got himself married, and all of a sudden was complaining how much more everything cost. (There's no record he ever found any treasure.) Pirates were still boldly rowing ashore in these parts to see what could be plundered; and smugglers used the coves as "roosts"; under cover of night they slipped in and out to sell goods to the folk of Long Island and thus escape paying duty to the Dutch.

Lady Deborah and Penelope never met up with any smugglers or pirates, but one day they had a scary encounter with a small party of Indians. Lulled into a sense of safety by the sight of miles of empty beach, they had walked quite some way from the protection of Richard and Sir-Harry at the pig farm. The day was hot and sunny, and both women carried parasols over their heads, pink-and-white ruffled affairs that Lady Deborah had ordered from England. Suddenly there emerged from the nearby woods three or four braves fearfully decorated with the black paint that meant they were on the warpath. For Penelope, it must have been an especially terrible moment in the light of her previous experience with Indian on a deserted beach. The wild men kept approaching; as Lady Deborah later wrote, "They looked as if they already had our scalps at their belts." The two women stood still, and neither screamed. The Indians came up, and then one of them reached out and took Penelope's parasol and examined it with the greatest curiosity. Lady Deborah, a teacher in her bones, pointed to the fiercely burning sun, then showed him how she stuck up the stretched cloth between herself and its rays. The Indian imitated her and the other men burst into laughter. Lady Deborah handed one of them her own parasol; then the two women turned and walked at a normal pace back down the beach, without looking back. Behind them came peal after peal of raucous laughter.

This episode served to lessen Lady Deborah's apprehension about Indians and other beachcombers, and soon thereafter she and Penelope dared cool themselves off by going wading in the crystal-clear water. "Surf bathing" in the ocean was such a novel idea at the time that the other women of Gravesend were scandalized when they heard that Lady Deborah and Penelope would do so. Besides the danger of crabs and even sharks, what did their menfolk think of women with their skirts hiked nearly to their knees, and coming home all wet and bedraggled? Lady Deborah said the men behaved as if they were envious, because their trousers prevented them from joining in the sport. And so, on many a summer's day in the 1640s could be seen two women wading in the blue shallows, probably the first white women to enjoy the waters at the beach that later Lady Deborah was to purchase from the Indians and name Coney Island.

"Conye's run and jump here," she wrote, referring to the rabbits on the island that were attracted to the vegetable mash fed to her pigs.

On May 11, 1647, Willem Kieft, for his "mishandling of the Indian situation, resulting in having to send for the English militia," was relieved of his post as Director General. By this time there had been so much fighting in the city of New Amsterdam that there were only one hundred people left in it. Under arrest, Kieft boarded the ship *Princess* which set sail for Amsterdam. The *Princess* went down with all hands lost.

Shortly thereafter Lady Deborah Moody made peace with the Indians, powwowing with several chiefs, and taking her turn with the peace pipe. The lands of Gravesend became Lady Deborah's in exchange for "one blanket, one gun and one kettle" to every Indian claimant. Nicholas Stillwell was present, protesting the giving out of guns. But Lady Deborah felt that an Indian with a musket was much more contented than an Indian without one, seeing them carried by other men.

All was again peace at Gravesend; yet hardly so back in England! In January of 1649 Charles I "laid his head on the stynking block in the Tower" at the order of Oliver Cromwell, who now led the country. England without a monarch! It seemed to Lady Deborah that the savage New World was no more bloody or unreliable than the Old. This turmoil affected all Europe and led to a dearth in the import of money. Metal coins became so scarce that the colonists were forced to go into the manufacture of wampum, offering "24 inches of white, 12 of purple beads, for one beaver skin." They found the Indians "hard to cheat, as in dealing with their own kind of money they are sharp as a pack of Arabs."

And now Quakers and Separatists began to arrive; they had heard of the religious freedom practiced as a matter of course at Gravesend and could not believe their ears, which had been so often in jeopardy in the Boston and Salem communities. In the finally rebuilt church, with its steeple hoisted aloft, the Puritans of Gravesend held services under their appointed minister on Sunday mornings at eleven. At twelve, the Separatists came in, with their own minister; and at one the Quakers might commune, without any minister at all. A certain six-footer named Andrew Crawford, of Scots origin, had been persecuted in Scotland, England, Boston, and Salem for attempting to put on the gray coat that was the badge of his faith and sit in a church with his fellows but without a preacher, praying silently and letting his body quake with emotion whenever the spirit moved him. Lady Deborah saw him in her church with his wife and children Sunday noons, tears of gratitude running down his leathery cheeks.

It was at one of these silent meetings that a man with a peg leg and a famous temper burst onto the Gravesend scene. He had been governor of Curaçao in the West Indies, where he had lost a leg in battle. Now he was the new director general of New Netherland, and he despised Quakers. Petrus Stuyvesant stood in the doorway of Lady Deborah's church and glowered at these ministerless Christians in their heretical gray. "Quakers!" he spat out, and, turning, stumped off to find the mayor of this unorthodox town.

He had heard that the mayor was a woman; still, even a weak-brained woman should not be forgiven for everything. By the time he had found Lady Deborah's house and been received in her parlor he was in a proper rage. After hearing his indignant expostulations, Lady Deborah gave back as good as she got. It was her town and if she wanted to give aid and comfort to Hottentots she had every right to do so. As for him, she had heard he had been the governor of Curaçao; did he consider the West Indians had no right to practice voodoo if they did no obvious harm with it? How much less violent were a group of Christians who never lifted a finger to harm a soul in their lives, and did not even try to coerce anybody into worshipping as they felt was right!

Before he could find any answers to all this, Lady Deborah invited Stuyvesant to the next town meeting, and said that "a short speech would be welcomed." She then sat him down in her kitchen with some fresh coffee and paper and pen. Petrus Stuyvesant must have realized early on that he had met his match.

At that town meeting was decided the future aims of Gravesend. "There shall be complete social, political and religious freedom. In agricultural and cultural development we shall open the door to wayfarers of whatever creed. . . .

Economic opportunity is held out." "We the People," said the charter of Gravesend, "shall make our own laws for our Quiet and Peaceful Existence." It was to be a hundred and twenty years before such words were used again, in the United States Constitution.

Petrus Stuyvesant made his short speech. "I shall govern you and the Indians as a father to his children, for the advantage of the chartered West India Company." Then he bent his torso in what might be called a bow in the direction of Lady Deborah. "And I wish a long and peaceful sojourn to this Lady Moody, without whom this town would not be—the Grande Dame of Gravesend."

So began a period of coexistence that was to be proved without parallel in the history of the English-Indians-Dutch in the 1600s. In 1654 Lady Deborah bought "Conye Island" from an Indian named Guttaquoh. She declared she knew it would become "a very popular community some day" because of its "beneficial sea airs and pleasant view."

A real test of white-copperskin relationship was made in October of 1650 when "a dreadful tempest unroofed houses, at Gravesend and in Indian villages, and dumped tons of hay from the fodder boats into the Bay." This time Indian and white worked together to clean things up; and when it was all over the Indians declared a festival at Gravesend. This turned out to be the third Thanksgiving held in the New World. For the feast Indians ran down that big bird with its greenish bronze and copper feathers, the wild turkey that few white men were fleet enough to capture. Indians brought the salmon and eels, whites contributed whole pigs and venison haunches roasted on open spits. Of course there was corn; and the Indians "served" it in a new way; they threw kernels into the fire; these popped with the sound of small-arms fire, but turned out to taste delicious. After the feast the Indians introduced some of their own games; in one of these a leather-skinned ball was carried and tossed from one team to another; in another, a stone was hit at by clubs and batted along the ground until it rested in the "camp" of the other team. At first the whites tried to take on the natives, but their efforts were so awkward that they earned the thigh-thumping Indian laughter and retreated smarting with humiliation—to practice these games among themselves after the festival was over.

In 1658 a flash fire swept through Gravesend, destroying several houses; and Petrus Stuyvesant decided to do something about fire prevention both at Gravesend and in New Amsterdam. He established the "Rattle Watch," in which men with buckets, in relays, patrolled the town from nine at night until the morning drumroll, carrying iron rattles; in case they spotted a fire they twirled these rattles by their handles, the clatter arousing all within hearing, and men would come running out in their nightgowns and caps, hurrying to the town pump to form a bucket-passing line. Stuyvesant also appointed a fire warden to go around inspecting the wooden chimneys of thatch-roofed houses, and if the owner was found with a dirty chimney where fire could get a start, he was fined three guilders; these proceeds were used to purchase more leather fire buckets from Holland.

"Peg Leg," as he was called, labored to prevent fires, but when they broke out he was usually among the first to appear on the scene, shouting instructions punctuated with the stomping of that wooden leg. For his obvious enjoyment of the excitement he had soon earned another nickname: "Old Fire Eater."

It was a good life, in Gravesend and New Amsterdam. And in 1659 it did not occur to Lady Deborah—or to Petrus Stuyvesant—that just five years from then an English fleet which had been building up its strength out on the Long Island would sail into New Amsterdam harbor and force Stuyvesant to hand over the city. Lady Deborah, herself the same age as the century, was in that year a contented woman, with grandchildren provided by her beloved Sir-Harry.

One morning Penelope Stout, carrying a picnic basket, came to the Dutch door of Lady Deborah's kitchen. The two had planned to go over to Coney Island for a lunch on the beach. Penelope pushed open the door to find Lady Deborah sitting in her rocking chair by the fireplace, apparently asleep. She had died peacefully some time in the night.

Her funeral was short and simple, and attended by her fellow Puritans, as well as Quakers, Separatists, Baptists, and Indians. Petrus Stuyvesant spoke briefly. "She was a grande dame from England," he said, "and a grande dame of Gravesend."

From the serenity of Gravesend we return briefly to Boston, a city fast approaching a state of civil riot. The Puritans were now beset on all sides by people clamoring for the right to live under God in ways other than the only one legally permitted, and they were not giving an inch. All that was needed to bring matters to a boil was one more incident of the nature of the banishment of Roger Williams or the murder of Anne Hutchinson. The Puritans versus everybody else—one of these factions must win, with irrevocable results.

Such an incident was to occur with the return of a woman still flaunting the Quaker gray that was like a red flag in the midst of the Puritan camp. She was that firebrand, Mary Dyer.

Part IV

OF TEARING DOWN

13

An Unlikely Saint

In 1643, when the Boston ministers came to Portsmouth, threatening to persecute Anne Hutchinson and her group still further if they didn't recant their heretical views, Mary Dyer and her husband William fled back to Providence and the relative protection of Roger Williams. It was in Providence that Mary heard of the massacre of Anne and her family.

Mary preached a moving funeral address in Providence. Then hearing expressions of satisfaction on the part of Governor Winthrop, she could not resist going to Boston. She addressed a large audience on the Common, and in scorching terms laid the guilt for these deaths at the door of the governor and his ministry. "She created a great scandal and was ordered to get out of town."

Mary got out. She went back to the place of her birth, London. She wanted to talk with any surviving relatives of Anne, and to see how Quakers were being treated in England. She found Katherine Scott, a sister of Anne, who told her that over a thousand Quakers were languishing in London jails, for having outraged both King Charles I and the Puritans by meeting without benefit of ministers and claiming they communicated directly with God.

Katherine Scott had become a Quaker, and dressed in the regulation habit of gray cloth gown, coat, and cap. Now Mary Dyer followed her example, making such an outfit for herself. And when she had put them on, all the old "firebrand" spirit in her passed away, leaving a calm resolution. Now she was a Quaker and only that, and the rest of her life would be devoted to working toward the day when all people might worship without other human beings or even a Book coming between themselves and their God.

Mary and Katherine Scott and Katherine's eleven-year-old daughter Patience came back to America with the intention of living as Quakers in the midst of the Puritans. They planned no marches or demonstrations, they would not even lift their voices. Instead, they considered that by the example of their quiet "friendly persuasion" they might awaken the Puritans to a realization of their own narrow interpretations of worship.

They arrived in Boston in 1656 at a very bad time. The Puritans felt themselves overrun by these anarchists who would do away with the ministry entirely—who would not worship in the Established Church or pay tithes to it, who would not take oaths or bear arms, who kept their hats on in the presence of magistrates and ministers and doffed them only when sitting in their strange, silent meetinghouses where, ostensibly praying directly to God, they were frequently raided and jailed. Even their speech was regarded as insulting: they said "thee" and "thou" instead of "you." The Puritans assumed this was to chastise *them* for not using the pronouns used in the Bible, whereas the Quakers said "thee" and "thou" out of their own complete honesty; "you," being either singular or plural, might possibly be misunderstood. No matter; everything a Quaker said or did was an irritant and a threat to the Puritan way of life. They were even beginning to appear at church services where, after the sermon, they would ceremoniously break bottles to demonstrate how empty they regarded its contents!

Mary Dyer and Katherine Scott missed by one day being seized and jailed right off the boat; the next day another boat-load of gray habits were given this treatment. But the following Sunday the two women and the girl were part of a group that slipped in at the back of a church and broke bottles after the sermon. Katherine Scott was seized, dragged out of the church by the infuriated minister and half the congregation, stripped to the waist, and whipped, while her daughter Patience and Mary Dyer looked on. All three had agreed that if any violence was done to them they would react with utter passivity.

Now they were told, "Get out of Boston and do not return, upon pain of worse." Mary took the Scotts home with her to Providence; then she returned. This time it was she who was stripped and whipped on the Common—"twenty stripes with a scourge of three cords." The crowd was restive and there were angry mutterings; there were many people even of the Puritan persuasion who did not relish the sight of a decent woman publicly humiliated and harmed. What was the world coming to?

Mary's husband came for her and took her back to Providence, pleading, for the sake of the normal children she had borne after "the monster," to remember her duties, if not as a wife, then as a mother. Mary did try, and for the next two years stayed home. But news from Boston steadily worsened. Imprisoned Quakers, the men at least, were having their ears cut off almost as a matter of routine, and branded with the S L of "seditious libeler" on their cheeks in the method of torture and shame learned so thoroughly from the mother country. And arriving Quakers were hauled off ships, examined for "witch marks," and put as prisoners on other ships heading for Barbados to be sold as slaves; the least violent treatment was having their bags and boxes searched and their books burned by the hangman in the marketplace. This book burning was presided over by the Reverend John Wilson, senior minister to John Cotton, a man who well remembered, from the trial of Anne Hutchinson, the name of Mary Dyer. Flinging the books into the flames, Wilson cried, "From the Devil they came, to the Devil they go!" In such times, a person of strong convictions just could not sit it out on the sidelines but had to stand up and be counted. Despite the danger, Mary decided to go back to Boston, if only to swell the ranks with the presence of one more anti-Puritan.

Hearing of this, however, the girl Patience determined to take Mary's place, trusting that her youth as well as her sex would save her from anything worse than a whipping, and she stole off to Boston with two men of the community, also Quakers. All were promptly jailed.

When Mary and Katherine heard of this, there was nothing to do but journey back to Boston and try to secure the girl's release. Instead, they themselves were thrown into prison. For the next three months they were kept in close confinement, without candles, and pen and ink denied them. They were not permitted to speak or be spoken to, and a board was nailed across the one window to keep anybody from so much as setting eyes upon them.

Finally they were let out of the cell and into a room containing instruments of torture. After being shown these instruments, they were released with the information that they were being spared this time because as women their ability to stir up discontent was negligible. No one heeded the opinions of women, but, because they were troublemakers, if they ever showed their faces in Boston again the Court would be obliged to treat them with the severity reserved for men.

Shortly thereafter, the two men who had been arrested

with Patience turned up in Providence to tell of fresh terrors. Now Quaker women were being seized, stripped to the waist, chained to the back of horse-carts, and whipped as they were dragged through the streets. There was a meeting at Mary Dyer's house, and then she made her decision. She and the two men would go back to Boston once again, and make the ultimate test of the Puritan law.

William Dyer was no more able to stop his wife in her headlong determination to sacrifice herself than Will Hutchinson had been able to alter the course of his wife's willful plunge into worse and worse situations.

Within a week of their arrival in Boston, Mary and her two companions were brought before a court and sentenced to be hanged. William Dyer was notified of his wife's impending death, and he began writing frantic and pleading letters to Boston officials, from whom he received no reply.

On a morning in 1659, Mary and the other two, dressed in their gray habits and wearing their hats, were taken from their cells and led to the place of execution, Boston Common. Beside the Frog Pond a stout elm (later called the "Great Tree") had been selected. A large crowd pushed and shoved for the best vantage point. The official in charge was the Reverend John Wilson. He bawled at the three of them:

"Shall such folk as you come before Authority with your hats on?"

They would. The two men were summoned ahead of Mary; it pained her to see that they were given no chance to make their small prepared speech about religious liberty to the assemblage. Each time they tried to raise their voices there was, at Wilson's command, a drumroll from the three soldier-drummers stationed nearby.

Each man in turn was blindfolded, a rope put around his neck, and then was made to climb the ladder beneath the outstretched limb of the tree, after which the ladder was pulled away. Both of the victims, Mary saw, died hard, the ladder having been removed too slowly, and the drop not violent enough to break the neck. She watched all this with a faraway feeling, as if it would not soon be happening to her. She was committed, already dead—even though she realized all their deaths would probably count for nothing.

The two men cut down finally and pronounced dead, Mary allowed the hands of the hangman to have at her person without protest. Her arms were bound behind her, her skirts tied around her ankles, her face was covered with Mr. Wilson's handkerchief, and she was lifted to the ladder.

At the top of the ladder she felt the noose tighten against her throat. Then she heard the drumroll; when it stopped she would be dropped.

It stopped. Mary Dyer stood on the ladder. And was not dropped! After a moment the rough voice of Wilson shouted, *Bring this one down!*

Hands were again upon her, awkwardly, on the ladder; and then she was standing before the Reverend Wilson, trying not to faint. He advised her that it had been intended to give her a severe scare. This had been her second and final act of charity. The Court did not want, if it could help it, "the notoriety of having to stop the mouth of a mere and foolish woman," but if Mistress Dyer were ever seen in the entire Massachusetts Bay Colony again, it would have no choice in the matter.

Suddenly there came news of a strange accident. The crowds that had come over from the mainland across the drawbridge had been thrown into confusion. "The drawbridge rose up and one end fell on many—one woman was killed." The Reverend Wilson was thoroughly shocked. Was this a sign of God's wrath at Mary Dyer's condemnation or at her reprieve? Whatever His meaning, best to get the woman out of the city first thing the next morning. She was bundled upon a horse, and word was sent ahead to have ready another horse at the boundary of the colony, to speed her back to Providence.

Mary, however, did not remain at home, where the temptation to give in and resume a quiet life might have been too strong, but sailed down the coast to Shelter Island, a small hamlet off Long Island where there was a settlement of Quakers. For the next few months she listened to reports of continued floggings, mutilations, and hangings. And then she could stand it no longer.

She went back, this time carrying a roll of clean linen under her arm. Brought before the court she was asked, "Are you not the woman who stood on the gallows, and was permitted to come down therefrom?"

"I am," she replied, "and I am back. This linen is for the wrapping of my body."

So Mary was again condemned to be hanged—at nine o'clock the next morning, upon that same tree on the Common. This time there were no others with her, and few people about to listen to her last words.

She stood on the ladder, blindfolded, and called out, "My life not availeth me in comparison to the liberty of the truth—" A little more was to come, but at that instant her body was dropped.

A woman had died in vain. Or had she?

In England in the first year of his reign, *Anno Domini* 1660, Charles II had taken as his motto the words of another Englishman, John Heywood: "New Broom sweepeth clean." One of his advisors was a Quaker named Edward Burrough. This man had just brought his monarch the latest news of atrocities perpetrated against Quakers in one of the American colonies. It was a long list of names and near the bottom, under "Hanged" was the name of Mary Dyer. Now, said Burrough, they were beginning to hang women!

"Your Majesty," said the advisor, "the Puritans there have a bad law. They will countenance no other form of worship but their own. They have opened a vein and blood is pouring out of it."

The king said, "I will stop that vein."

And he did. Thousands of Quakers were let out of jails in both England and New England, and stern edicts were published against their further persecution. The year 1660 was the beginning of the end of Puritan intolerance and the iron grip of theocracy.

Even more than she had dared to dream, the firebrand-turned-calm-martyr had achieved her longed-for ends.

Today, across from Boston Common, on the hilly eminence of the State House, two statues flank the entrance, beneath the great gilded dome. The figure of Mary Dyer is seated, in her Quaker habit, hands folded in the attitude of those who may protest but contemplate no violence. The plaque on her pedestal reads: "Witness for religious freedom, hanged on Boston Common 1660" and her last words are quoted. Anne Hutchinson is her companion, shown standing and with her hand on the shoulder of her daughter Susannah. Her plaque: "Killed Eastchester 1643. A courageous exponent of civil liberty and religious tolerance."

Sir Henry Vane, too, has found his niche, greeting visitors to the Boston Public Library, where he looms larger than life in his plumed tricorne, neat beard, and spurred boots. No doubt he would like to have remained on in the state where he had been so easily elected second governor, perhaps even to break that shaky charter that stretched "from Sea to Sea." But Anne's trial had fixed his star upon another course; the charter remained unbroken (after the Revolution, in 1783, Massachusetts sued to obtain its lawful territories of Michigan and Wisconsin!) and the plaque at the base of Sir Henry's statue records the fact of his beheading in London in 1662—

also the remark of the man responsible for his banishment, John Winthrop, and sounding rather apologetic: "He stirred himself up such friends."

And what of that eleven-times governor of Massachusetts? His granite likeness, standing in the suppliant pose of a servant of the people, stood for years on the grounds of the First Church of Boston, on a quiet residential corner in Back Bay. In 1968 the church was rent by an explosion and fire, and the statue was blown off its pedestal. Two years later the blackened brick shell of the church still remains, as well as the pedestal marked *John Winthrop*, around which are scattered great chunks of stone. In the placid, respectable place the sight is so incongruous as to be unsettling, as if the spirit of those other untidy times had broken through and would not go away, to remind a twentieth-century Boston, center of culture and reason, of its violent beginnings.

Mary Dyer, calm martyr, started out as a gadfly. "That Cotton is a trimmer." "Make the ministers swear." Perhaps her name persists in a similar manner; it must keep Boston postmen on the alert with Dyer Street, Dyer Court, and Dyer Avenue. As for Anne Hutchinson, a direct descendant, Thomas, became the last royal governor before the Revolution; like his famous ancestor, he believed in defending his convictions. In 1773 all Boston was up in arms over the British import tax on tea. When three tea-laden ships sailed into the harbor, Governor Hutchinson had a group of colonists, among them Samuel Adams and Paul Revere, disguise themselves as Indians, board the ships at night, and throw the tea overboard, an event that became known as the Boston Tea Party. One believes Anne would have approved of that: justice done and no blood shed!

Part V

TOWARD FUTURES

14

"And She as Good as Dead"

Having survived being scalped, partially disemboweled, and her shoulder slashed at age twenty-two, Penelope Stout may have felt that the rest of her life seemed positively charmed. In the hostile environment of the 1600s in America there was always somebody around to save her life.

The old Lenni Lenape, Tisquantum, had managed this feat twice—once when he had her patched up by his squaws after the scalping, and again when he had come to Gravesend to warn her of the Indian uprising. Next in order of Penelope-savers came a midwife named Trijn Jonas, a Dutch woman from New Amsterdam, who came over on the Bruijkleen ferry to assist at the delivery of Penelope's first child—a difficult birth—and stemmed a hemorrhage, saving both mother and child. Her advice was, "No more birthings for you, mistress, you ain't got the stamina for 'em."

The baby, born in 1645, was named John. John did not have a lonely childhood. After him came Richard, James,

Mary, Alice, Peter, Sarah, Jonathan, David, and Benjamin.

Her third and last lifesaver was Dr. Roger Parke.

After the death of Lady Deborah Moody, Penelope and her family left Gravesend with regret and rowed across the water to New Jersey, where there was more land available, and richer soil, for the growing of tobacco. They bought a large area in Monmouth County; and having discovered under Lady Deborah's "permissive" religious ways that they were of the Baptist persuasion, they called the village they founded Baptist Town (later Middletown) and built the first Baptist church in New Jersey there.

In their early years in Baptist Town there were very few other white settlers. Red men thickly populated the forests with their wigwams and held powwows on the banks of the nearby brook. And in all the square miles of wilderness between the New York area and the Swedish settlement later to become Philadelphia, there roamed just one non-Indian doctor—and, as Dr. Parke was the first to admit, Indians had taught him all the medicine he knew. A tall, loose-jointed bag of skin and bones, Parke maintained a sort of peregrinating round up and down New Jersey, through which ran not a single road. Over hills and through woods went Parke, carrying in his saddlebags the only "drug store" to be found in hundreds of miles.

Parke was very glad to see the Stout family—all those new people with whom to speak English! He proudly showed off his stock, giving a spiel he had developed about his "plasters and poultices, pills and powders, for pukes and purges." Also, he sold "Old Doc Parke's Yarbs," bitter-tasting concoctions of herbs for the curing of constipation, "washes" (liniments), rosemary water for a stinking breath, rocket flowers for unseemly smelling armpits, white-flowered yarrow to stop the shedding of hair and for backaches, nettles to strengthen weary limbs and stir up lust, yellow tansy to prevent worms and miscarriages, white feverfew for attacks of the black melancholy, poppy seed (steeped in your own wine) to help cure nightmares, dandelion stems for giddiness of the brain, wild thyme for relief from frenzy, and house leek to fend off lightning. Few of these homeopathic helps were needed by the generally healthy Stouts, but at the end of an especially hard winter, that of 1665, Penelope came down with pneumonia. She lay in bed gasping for breath, and in desperation Richard Stout set out to find the self-taught old quack who was the only hope in the territory.

"Parke?" he called to Indians. "Old-Doc-Parke?" They knew the name. Some waved Richard in the right direction.

On the third day he found the doctor who himself had found a new fishing stream and didn't particularly want to leave it to the Indians. They would drag it with nets, and by the time he got back there wouldn't be anything left . . . but he came along. Richard urged his own horse ahead, over the rocks and briary hills. He expected to find a dead wife when he got back.

Penelope was still hanging on, but from the terrible racking sound of her breathing, her lungs had filled with fluid. Dr. Parke took one look and began rolling up his sleeves. He looked positively cheerful. It seemed he had been waiting for years for the opportunity to try out his "sweating stones."

One can imagine the husband's dismay as preparations were carried out. First Dr. Parke sold him some heavy fur skins, which had to be sewn together to form a tent—the older children were put to work on that task. Then a large stone was heated and placed inside this tent of skins. Meanwhile Parke brewed up a jug of "boneset tea," which he managed to get down Penelope's throat—this was to bring on sweating. After that, her clothes were removed and she was placed inside the tent, where soon her body broke out into a sweat. Dr. Parke was pleased. Now take out the patient, and plunge her into the icy waters of the nearby pond! Richard protested, but Parke was adamant. Venture all or gain nothing!

The third and final part of the treatment was to wrap the sufferer in a heavy blanket and put her back in bed.

She recovered.

After that, Dr. Parke was an honored guest in the household, along with another old "original," the ubiquitous Tisquantum. The Lenni Lenape chief was now over seventy, and he behaved as if he were lonely. He would appear in Penelope's front yard with some small gift, a wooden bowl hollowed into the shape of a turtle, or, upon the birth of a new baby, a ceremonial doll. The doll would protect the child's health, he warned, only if it were given a ceremonial dance and new clothes every spring; and it should be addressed as "Grandmother." Penelope gravely followed instructions; during her years of association with Indians she had come gradually to respect many of their strange prescriptions.

Whenever Tisquantum visited, he was invited to share the evening meal, and on such occasions his leathery face with its rows of deep vertical wrinkles would break into an unaccustomed smile. The meal usually centered around the stewpot, called the "loblolly," because that was the sound heard in its bubbling contents. As Penelope wrote, "All hands dipped into the loblolly pot at once, and some times two or three of us would catch hold of the same wanted piece." The old chief relaxed in Penelope's kitchen with its delft-blue tiles framing the fireplace—and kept up with his English. A *man* still had to defend himself with the white man. In recent years he had picked up the habit of sighing. Long, deep sighs would come from his lips as he sat in Penelope's kitchen after dinner, drawing on his pipe. She knew this meant he was troubled and would wait for him to find the words to express his feelings. One such time was about "The Walking Agreement." The white skins had tricked the "men" once more. The Lenni Lenape had put their mark to a contract to sell some of their land, in which the agreement had been "land as far as a man can walk in a day and a half," and instead of walking, the white skins had *run!* Penelope wrote, "One dared not laugh," but she must have been sorely tempted; how like her fellow whites!

Another thing that puzzled and worried Tisquantum was the change in authority in "New Amsterdam." Now that the English had bested the Dutch, he could see more clearly than before that his country was being divided and settled by more than one "tribe" of white skins. Penelope could be of no help. She too sensed that the English and Dutch, French and Swedes would slowly, steadily, and inexorably push the Indians aside. She could not even say whether this was right or wrong, good or bad; it simply *was*. She herself had come from a tiny country where the sea was forever encroaching, and the inhabitants had got together with a single-minded will to push it back. She saw no such single determination on the part of Indians toward the goal of pushing back the whites. In spite of the growing threat, Indians still thought in terms of their own "nation," tribes within this nation, villages within this tribe. Tisquantum was unhappy about the English and Dutch, but his most bitter enmity lay coiled like a rattler against his blood enemy, the Mohawks of the Long Island branch of the Iroquois!

Richard Stout's growing tobacco business took him to New York about twice a year, and in 1670, when their youngest child, Benjamin, was about eight months old, Penelope gathered together all ten of her children and came along. She was curious to see how the city had changed under the English, and, too, she needed all sorts of new things. She found that New York had burgeoned since she had seen it last at the time of her marriage in the fort and short honeymoon in that original windmill; both fort and windmill were still a part of the scene. She also found a bewildering profusion of the goods and services she needed. Still working as a seamstress, and inducting her teen-aged daughter Alice (Alse) into the trade, Penelope found this selection:

"Nun-Thread, Nun-Cloth, Nankeens, Bed-Ticks, Ravens-duck and Cambric Tabbies, Shalloons for Muffs and Tippets, Ticklenburghs, fourteen butts of Best Holland Geneva and Twenty Tons of Fustick."

And as a housewife, displayed for her choice: "Barrels of Brimstone, Bladders of Snuff, Boxes of Tooth-Ache Cure, Bushels of Nuts, Bales of Black Pepper, Bays of Ginger. Quarter-Casques of Whale Oil, Firkins of Butter and Lard . . . Hogsheads of Tallow, Quintels of Codfish, Pipes of Sherry, Puncheons of Rum, Parcels of Hides, Loads of Lamp Black, Tierces of Tobacco, and Anchors, for the making of Nails."

Penelope was now in need of another "slavy"; the young Negro girl she had bought for several pounds three years ago had herself married, her husband having bought her off; and so she was in need of another girl to help her with the cooking. And she could use a wet nurse for Benjy, children not usually being weaned before they were eighteen months or more. A woman with ten children needed all sorts of help! And so she and Alice consulted the signs of sales and services posted all around the bustling marketplace:

TO BE SOLD
A Pair of Bay Horses,
Well Used to the Sleigh,
AND
A Smart Likely Negro Wench
who understands plain Cooking.

WET NURSE
A young Woman with a fine
Breast of Milk, would wish
to take a Gentleman's
Child to Suckle.

Penelope made notes of all the Negro wenches and wet nurses; Richard would have to decide on all that later. Some of the Negro cooks could not be sold without the acquisition also of the horses—and so this was a man's decision.

But one advertisement was clearly a woman's decision—so decided Penelope Stout and her daughter Alice:

> National Smith, Perfumer from London offers his exquisite Pomades and Perfume, also begs to acquaint the Ladies that he has killed a fine fat BEAR, and such as are desirous of having any of the Grease will be pleased to send their servants to cut it off, at 35 pence per portion.

Mother and daughter went off forthwith to find this National Smith. They both had the dry skin of natural blondes, and had suffered for years from the "tight" feeling brought on by extremes of hot and cold climate. The New World was hardly a tropical balm for a woman's skin!

They bought a slab of bear grease and wandered back again to the marketplace, awaiting Richard, and taking turns rubbing the soothing fat into forehead and cheeks. And sharing it with other women shoppers. Ah, what bliss!

By 1675 Richard Stout and his sons owned some 780 acres of fertile New Jersey farmland—"marl," it was called, rich in lime, clay, and potash. Middletown had grown up around the Stouts; and Richard was elected to the office of overseer, member of the Constable Court, and an Indian commissioner. In 1682 he attended a conference at which a respected Indian chief, called by the whites "Tammany," made a pact with the Englishman William Penn; the agreement led to the establishment of the City of Brotherly Love, Philadelphia.

The French-Indian wars broke out in 1689; the following year the first newspaper in America was born—and promptly banned. It was called *Publick Occurrences*, and its reason for existence: "That Memorial Occurents of Divine Providence may not be neglected or forgotten, as they too often are. It is designed that the country shall be furnished with a News Paper once a month (or if any Glut of Occurrence happen, oftener)." The first issue was filled not so much with matters of divine providence as the fact that Governor Winthrop ("Fitz-John," grandson of the founder of Boston) had tried to buy the aid of the Mohawk Indians at a certain price per scalp, to help him kill off the French in Canada—the Mohawks had begged off, pleading an epidemic of smallpox the whites had brought them—and this news in a public paper caused it to be burned as fast as it appeared; anyone caught selling or reading it was to be prosecuted.

In 1705, at the age of ninety-five, Richard Stout succumbed. His wife wrote a single line, "I was never unhappy with him." Perhaps there has never been a better tribute.

She was now herself aged seventy-three, a frail woman but still clear-eyed, interested in the progress of her grandchildren. And so she lived on. And on, and on! She who had been born when William Shakespeare was only six years in the grave, endured to see the city of Philadelphia rise, and the beginnings of democracy put down their tentative roots.

She was a hundred and ten when she died in 1732, and was buried beside her husband on a farm three miles west of the village of Middletown. She left over five hundred descendants.

As one of them said, "All these sprang from one woman, and she as good as dead."

They come together now, every year in September, these descendants of Penelope Stout. From all over the country they converge on Hopewell Township, New Jersey, to celebrate their uncommon ancestors. Among them they represent a cross section of America. There is Jimmy Stout, retired as a jockey in 1954 after twenty-four years of racing, and named to the Hall of Fame in Saratoga Springs. There was William

Bushnell Stout, who helped design the Liberty airplane engine of World War I, and a pioneering high-speed railroad car in the 1930s. A horticultural member of the clan was Dr. A. B. Stout, for thirty-five years on the staff of the New York Botanical Garden, and pioneer hybridizer of the day lily. Perhaps the best-known contemporary relative is the mystery writer, Rex Stout, creator of "Nero Wolfe."

And there they are, those four women who had a voice in America's beginnings—Anne Hutchinson and Mary Dyer, whose protests against religious intolerance helped achieve freedom of worship and speech, Lady Deborah Moody, whose interest in building a town combined with a live-and-let-live outlook rare in those rigid times; and Penelope Stout, who had her full share of misfortunes, and survived them. Perhaps all together they represent the finest strains that wove into the making of American womanhood. Or perhaps they ought to be seen as just four individuals, each coming to terms with the world as she saw it.

And leaving it a little better place to live in.

Sources and Readings

ALEXANDER, WILLIAM T. *History of the Colored Race in America*. Kansas City, Mo.: Palmetto Publishing Company, 1881.

BOLTON, R. P. *A Woman Misunderstood*. New York: Schoen Printing Company, 1931.

BRADFORD, WILLIAM. *History of Plimouth Plantation*. Boston: Houghton, Mifflin & Co., 1896.

FLICK, ALEXANDER C. *Lady Deborah Moody, Grand Dame of Gravesend*. Brooklyn, published by the author, 1939.

GORGES, SIR FERDINANDO. *America Painted to the Life*. London, published by the author, 1659.

HARRINGTON, M. R. *Indians of New Jersey—Dickon Among the Lenapes*. New Brunswick, N.J.: Rutgers University Press, 1963.

JACKSON, BIRDSALL. *How They Lived—Old Long Island Tales*. Rockville Centre, N.Y.: Paumanok Press, 1941.

McCULLOUGH, EDO. *Good Old Coney Island*. New York: Charles Scribner's Sons, 1957.

OVERTON, JACQUELINE. *Long Island's Story*. Port Washington, N.Y.: Ira J. Friedman, Inc., 1929, 1961.

RUGG, WINIFRED K. *Unafraid, A Life of Anne Hutchinson.* Boston and New York: Houghton-Mifflin Company, 1930.

SMITH, SAMUEL. *The History of the Colony of New Jersey.* Burlington, N.J.: J. Parker, 1765.

STOKES, ISAAC NEWTON PHELPS. *The Iconography of Manhattan Island.* New York: R. H. Dodd, 1915–1928.

WINTHROP, JOHN. *A Journal.* Hartford: Elisha Babcock, 1790.

Index

DATE DUE